THE POWER OF PLAY AND LEARNING

THE POWER OF PLAY &LEARNING

MaryJane Devlin

Susan H.D. Argyros
Elizabeth A. Devlin

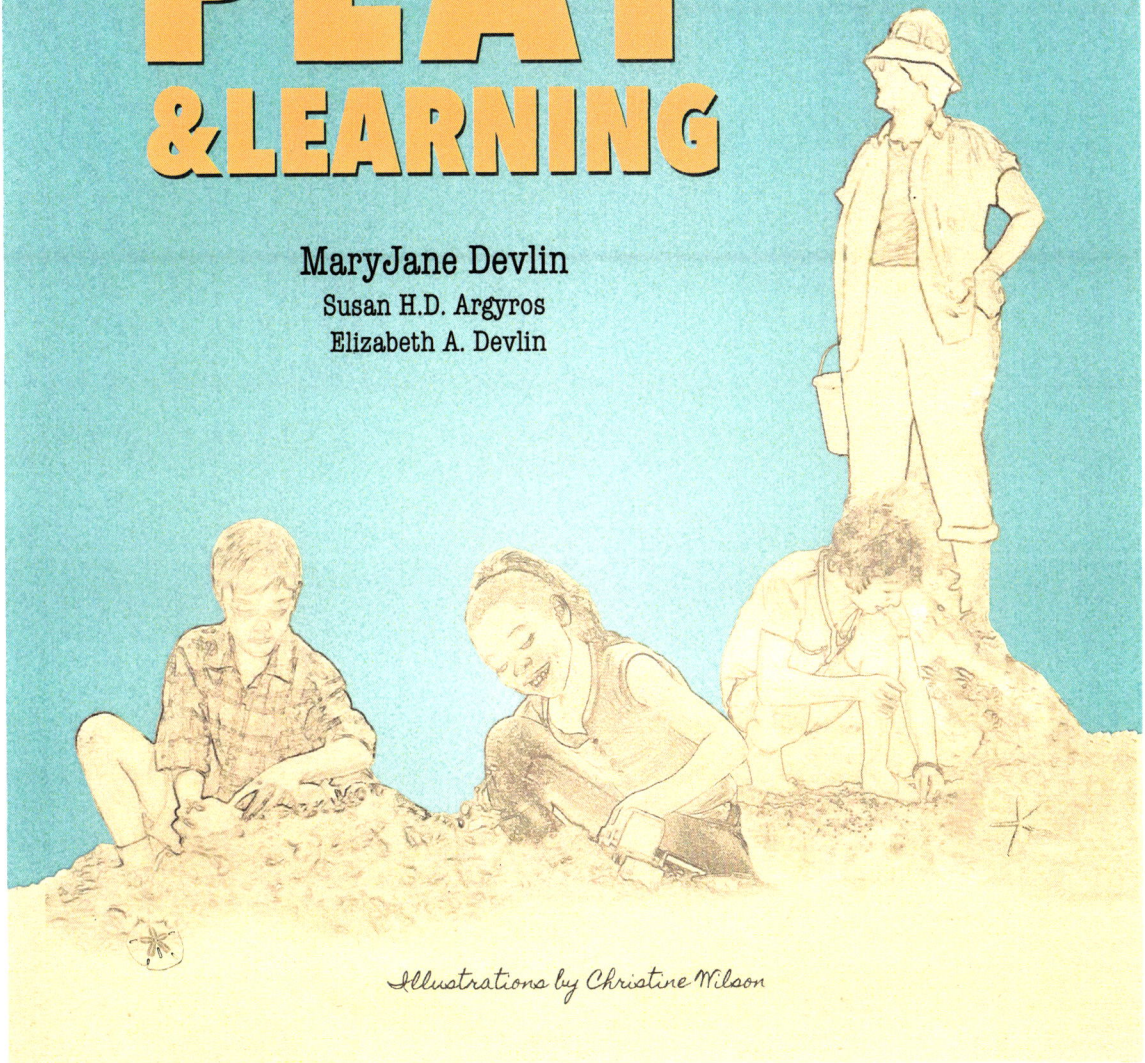

Illustrations by Christine Wilson

Haley's
Athol, Massachusetts

Haley's
488 South Main Street
Athol, MA 01331
haley.antique@verizon.net
800.215.8805

Layout designed in collaboration with
Susan H. D. Argyros and Elizabeth A. Devlin.

Copy edited by Mary-Ann DeVita Palmieri.

Photos from the authors' collection.
Back cover photo by Susan Brown Devlin.

Library of Congress Cataloging-in-Publication Data
Names: Devlin, MaryJane, author. | Devlin, Elizabeth A., author. | Argyros,
    Susan H.D., author.
Title: The power of play and learning / MaryJane Devlin with Elizabeth A.
    Devlin, Susan H.D. Argyros : illustrated by Christine Wilson.
Description: Athol : Haley's, [2018] | Includes bibliographical references.
Identifiers: LCCN 2018025867 | ISBN 9781948380010
Subjects: LCSH: Play. | Child development. | Kindergarten--Activity programs.
    | First grade (Education)--Activity programs.

to my husband, Lee, for all his love and support

to my children,
Chris, Bill, Susan, Elizabeth, Maura

to my daughters-in-law and sons-in-law
Sue, Joan, David, Tom

to my grandchildren,
Aaron, Paul, Jesse, Leslie, Megan, Liam, Tara,
Derek, Ana, David, Owen, Shanna

to my great grandchildren,
Liliana, Amaya, Ariana, Nicholas, Grace,
Shawn, Abel, Corey, Jackson, Colin,
and those yet to come . . .

to my former students
and children in schools today

May you all know life filled with love and play.

Play is the rehearsal of life's meaning, the crystallization of

knowing, understanding, creating, and being.

It is ever changing, adapting, reflective, and exciting.

"Please, give us time to play," our children are pleading.

"Please give us time to be curious, to explore, and

to make mistakes." Play turns inquiring minds into

critical thinkers, designers, and creators.

—MaryJane Devlin

Contents

Photos

A Classroom Where We Can Gain Vivid and Truthful Knowledge

a foreword by John Coe

It is all too rare for us to read a book which describes the work of a dedicated and successful teacher, and this foreword prefaces such a book and cherishes its value. More usually books about education are written by academics and, indeed, their words are often important to those who teach. But nothing can match the impact of the reality of the classroom, the interchange between people young and old, the working out of ideas translated into what actually happens, and the way that caring concern, difficult if not impossible to research, colors and shapes the teacher's work.

MaryJane Devlin is first and foremost a practitioner and, with the help of her family, has given us a book that takes us into her classroom where we can gain vivid and truthful knowledge of what it is really like to be taught by her. The experience of teaching draws upon the insights of academics and the results of their research, but all is transmuted into reality through the human presence of the teacher.

The learning and teaching described can be positioned firmly within the traditions of kindergarten education in the developed world. It was entirely understandable that a process of education that places the child at the center began with the youngest children. You can't overlook the nature of five-year-olds. Here they are, bursting with energy, always on the move, trying out new skills with every new day, and learning at a rate never matched in later life —learning though the naturalness of living which for them is called play. How absurd would it be, said the early pioneers, for us to try to sit the children down in serried ranks, to shut them up and stop them learning so well and so richly because they have to listen quietly to the instructive words of the teacher. So it was that active, fully experiential learning began with the youngest children, and so it is that such teaching and learning continues with great success to the present day.

It was some sixty years ago that teachers in the USA and in Britain began actively to question why grade-school education should differ so markedly from the child-centered practice of the kindergarten. The growth of children is gradual and evolutionary. They don't turn into different beings immediately on becoming six years old, and they don't turn suddenly into meek and passive learners required only to sit still, denying their nature as they are taught by rote rather than learning through experience.

The methods of the kindergartens began to move upwards through the grades. Of course, education in the first and successive grades was not precisely similar to the kindergarten. As children gained skills, so their new proficiencies became part of school life, but the essential point remained. Children were at the heart of the learning process. The curriculum, objectives, learning environment, and role of the teacher were matched to the nature of the child rather than the reverse which formerly had been typical of grade-school education. For at least a quarter of a century, the evolutionary development of elementary education progressed as changes rooted in the kindergarten moved upwardly through the school system. Some farsighted schools even questioned the lock-step dominance of the grades. Children are not growing and changing in line abreast; each one is unique, and education that recognizes and acknowledges that uniqueness should be cautious about an organization that assumes that all the children of eight years old are ready for the same challenge to their understanding and emerging skill. This led to the creation of vertically grouped or multi-aged classes, which mirrored the success already evidenced in small schools where such organization had long been the practice.

Sadly, the progress was not to last. Gifted teachers continued to receive the support of the families they served and their local communities, but larger, more powerful forces began to intervene in the classroom.

Governments, challenged by international competiveness, woke up to the vital need for a skilled workforce, and the pressure they began to apply was rooted in a concern for the educational standards achieved by young people at the end of formal education. The first survey of standards by the Programme for International Student Assessment (PISA) was published in the year 2000, and for the first time, countries were ranked in league tables. Downward pressure was exerted on school systems, and it had an undoubted effect upon teachers of young children. They, too, found their teaching judged through publication of league tables that set school against school. The purpose of early education was upended—the system demanded to know how well schools are preparing children for the later stages of education and not how well schools are meeting the needs of children as they teach them today. Teachers know that the best way of preparing for tomorrow is to live and learn in the present, but such longer term professionalism has not appealed to those who seek immediate results.

The main impact of national accountability has been on the quality of education and its relevance to life's demands. For too many years, the evaluation of standards has focused upon the core of the curriculum. Literacy and numeracy are held to be essential to future progress, and performance in tests of these areas of the curriculum has dominated the work of schools. The result has been a narrowing of children's experience of learning and, equally damaging, an undue concentration upon the skills which are testable and a neglect of the application of skill which is the ultimate aim of our teaching.

The exponential growth of digital technology, with computing power doubling every eighteen months, has compounded the harmful emphasis upon test results. Computers can handle vast amounts of data with ease, and data such as test results are necessarily expressed in stark binary terms. So, the tests have required simple right or wrong answers to questions and have neglected the human and more complex subtleties of the teacher's knowledge of the child.

So, for child-centered teachers like MaryJane Devlin, the educational sky has been dark for a good number of years. Seeing the benefits to their children, parents have rallied behind teachers who have had to defend the integrity of their work while mitigating the worst aspects of the test-driven school life required by society.

But now at last, at long last, there are the first real signs that the sky is beginning to lighten. The More-Than-a-Score movement, begun in 2014, brings together teachers and parents who want more for their children than the narrowness of mere preparation for tests. They call for a process of education that includes vitally important human attributes such as resource-fulness, creativity, persistence, curiosity, and critical thinking and that puts the developing nature of the learner at the center of the teacher's concern. There has been too much for the test and not enough for the child.

Evidence from research that can no longer be ignored shows that schools with the widest and most challenging curriculum achieve the highest standards. The wide-ranging approach of MaryJane Devlin's kindergarten provides a model to be followed for older children, and this is the way to higher achievement in the core skills.

The most recent PISA international assessment published in 2015 moves on from its focus on the core of the curriculum to acknowledge the changing climate of thought by including students' well-being as important to the survey. Increasingly, and this is of the greatest significance, the corporate world of industry and commerce has begun to prioritize personal qualities in school leavers as they enter the world of work. The next twenty years will see routine work and routine thinkers replaced by robots, and education has begun to respond to the challenge.

The sky is lighter, and the coming years are full of promise. "More for the children and less for the test." That is MaryJane Devlin's mantra that readers of this book will carry with them as they go forward.

Young Minds at Work

a preface by Susan H. D. Argyros

Step over the threshold into Mrs. Devlin's kindergarten and first-grade classroom, and you will see areas of stuff inviting minds to come play, work, and learn. No rows or circles of desks face the place where a teacher would stand. No shelves of identical practice books with names on the covers are in piles on shelves. Step into the classroom, and you will see spaces set up as invitations to learn, explore, and investigate. Look one way, and you will see dress-up costumes, a listening center, and carrots and potatoes growing on the windowsill. Look the other way, and there will be buckets of rocks, sand, magnets, and water for science experiments. Another space will store math manipulatives, writing supplies, and building blocks. Shelves with labeled bins and lots of books will be around the room. Take a panoramic view of this classroom, and you will see fully engaged five-, six- and seven-year-olds in a landscape of opportunities to be intellectual, social, loving, and happy learners together.

> *Somewhere amidst the sea of movement, you will see Mrs. Devlin . . . facilitating active learning.*

Somewhere amidst the sea of movement, you will see Mrs. Devlin, their teacher and our mother, facilitating active learning. There, in the midst of young minds at work, she observes the successes and challenges of her students, thinks about their needs, and plans their next lessons. MaryJane Devlin was a teacher way ahead of her time for teaching young children to be curious about learning, to think critically, and to be self-sufficient in leading their own learning.

As many teachers turned to workbooks with scripted programs, Mom slid worksheets into plastic sleeves for students to practice a skill, not as an end-all-be-all, and never for a grade. She saw worksheets as busy work and not important in developing thinkers who can solve problems. She understood that children learn more if allowed to discover on their own or practice skills in ways that would more fully engage the learner. Forming letters in the sand or in the air is much more fun than tracing dotted lines on worksheets and leads to learning for the long term.

Mom had a presence; she was the conductor in charge. Using her voice to guide her students, she moved seamlessly from one activity to another. She sang to get everyone's attention with a voice that could project to every corner of the room. To transition from Choice Board time to Physical Education, she sang, and as if following the Pied Piper, children stopped working and began singing along as they moved to the circle of rug squares in the front of the room. Mom stopped singing and announced firmly they would leave for the gym in five minutes, then sang:

"Clean up, clean up. Everybody clean up." On cue, students sang and moved to clean up their areas. Soon the song turned to "Line up, line up. Everybody line up." Mom loved to sing.

Mrs. Devlin's room was bustling. She welcomed parents and volunteers to share their knowledge and expertise and didn't hesitate to assign someone to work with a group on a project in the hall or read a story to a child. A pleased parent wrote about Mom in the local newspaper:

> A special note to Mrs. Devlin, kindergarten teacher, for her tireless, imaginative efforts in class and her quiet yet firm discipline and loving attention given to her students.

When our dad retired, he suddenly was available to chaperone field trips and help in the classroom with bigger projects such as building the *Mayflower* out of refrigerator boxes. He helped the children construct a bow for the ship after cutting the wood. Even though he was not a teacher by profession, our dad likes to share his own teaching stories and tease Mom about how she always gave him the more active kids to look after.

When Mom retired, education was marching toward measuring learning with standardized tests. Like many effective teachers, she saw no solid evidence to connect higher test scores with an ability to think creatively and critically. Mom's data showed her students did as well as or better on standardized tests than students in traditional classrooms, yet she was certain her students had more fun learning.

Our mom wrote *The Power of Play and Learning* over the course of many years. We took her drafts and notes to complete her dream of sharing her beliefs on childhood, learning, and play. In writing her book, Mom referred to her ideas as recipes for learning because, like chefs, teachers need to add their own passion and personal touch. Mom's love for learning transcended to her students and her own children. Her message about play is as timely today as it was a hundred years ago. In the following chapters, she shows us there *is* power in play.

Lee Devlin, left rear, chaperones a field trip to Hammonasset State Park as children listen to his wife and their teacher, MaryJane Devlin, share her knowledge about ocean life.

Children Need Play

an introduction by MaryJane Devlin

Children have energy to play and need to play. Playing in school has become endangered and deemed a frivolity and superfluous. Yet, play is a necessity. To ignore nature's way of teaching and learning prevents passing on a natural way of learning to our future generations. Play is a child's way of learning. It reveals an attitude that fuels the desire to learn. Play is crucial to a child's full development and well-being. Children need believers, articulators, and advocates to put children's play back in its proper place in childhood.

When educational approaches neglect play and measure academic achievement solely by mastery of discrete skills on statistically normed tests, instead of demonstrated behaviors, we harm children's learning. A test score sadly becomes more important than the learner. Such an approach does not take into account the whole child's emotional, social, and developmental needs, which are paramount to a successful, healthy life.

> *Parents, teachers, and communities have a responsibility for the care of each child's soul, spirit, and body.*

Parents, teachers, and communities have a responsibility for the care of each child's soul, spirit, and body, respectively, as they mature. In order to engage in competition for academic excellence, some school districts have curtailed or even eliminated the arts and physical education. Providing time for arts and physical education helps children care about themselves and others. Without our commitment to ensure the nature of caring, our culture may not endure nor our children thrive.

Play primarily enables children to make sense of their ever-changing world and their place in it. As adults, we realize the necessity to unwind, enjoy humor, engage in relationships, exercise our bodies, and reflect on our

Using cardboard, students design and create a vehicle.

thoughts about experiences. We allow ourselves time to "play" in consideration of our health, both physically and spiritually. We understand that play is important with regard to our competency, productivity, and survival. Oliver Wendell Holmes said, "We do not quit playing because we grow old; we grow old because we quit playing." When opportunities to play become limited, we deny children a healthy balance in a growing technological world. Strong bodies, spirits, and minds, essential in a balanced life, require caring and thoughtful building. Children figure out their world through play.

Broad, mandated curricular objectives and constant standard measures can leave teachers little time to cover all of the requirements and little time for children to have personal choice in what they want to learn. On the other hand, mandated curricular objectives can be met by filling the child's day with opportunities to communicate, sing, read, write and tell stories, explore, memorize, imagine, plan, record, calculate, reflect, and experience the world through play. Children will not only achieve targeted learning objectives, but they will also succeed far beyond our expectations.

Playtime in school enhances learning through the arts, music, and academics. During play, there is an impetus toward construction of new knowledge from the children crafting and sharing ideas that will lead toward task mastery. More importantly, the children will not feel stressed while reaching their fullest potential.

During my public school teaching career, I was fortunate to be a member of a group of teachers who developed and implemented a program called the Integrated Day Program (multi-grade groups of K-1, 2-3 and 4-5). This program was a school-within-a-school program where learning experiences vary for each student based on individual needs, interests, and developmental capacities. We built the Integrated Day Program on the premise that the child must be an active participant in his or her learning in a rich environment filled with hands-on materials and thematically based activities. The ultimate goal of the program was to develop informed, thinking citizens capable of contributing to and effectively participating in society.

The program included built-in time for all Integrated Day teachers across the grade levels to meet to review and assess the effectiveness of the program. The integrity of the program depended on collaboration time. Integrated Day Program teachers observed and noted what children learned through photos, artifacts, and anecdotes. Students participated in mandated norm-referenced standardized tests. Student literacy skills were also measured with criterion-referenced tests.

We developed our Integrated Day Program by studying similar initiatives such as those of John Coe, a British primary education specialist who states, "Experience is the great teacher of the young. We must give our children room to grow and engage in learning on their own."

> *Child-centered learning that focuses on play provides food for the body, food for the intellect, and food for the spirit.*

Child-centered learning that focuses on play provides food for the body, food for the intellect, and food for the spirit. Play enhances morality, character, responsibility, kindness, and manners. Because the teacher facilitates students at play and students control the means and goals of play, it can be viewed as an inherently creative activity, one that cultivates flexible, divergent thinking. With intention, time to play is a gift to open doors and minds to critical thinking, so essential to our future inventors, scientists, and leaders. When we don't provide time for play, we starve our world's future promise.

Integrated Day teachers invited parents to come into the classroom and encouraged them to support education in various ways. Parent participation was an integral component. Parents went on field trips related to our research-inquiry study; they came into the classroom to share their knowledge; and they supported their children by attending presentations and displays of culminating projects. I kept parents informed of our learning focus. Students also had an important role through facilitating and sharing what they had learned with their parents and other students.

Play in a classroom embraces the need for order and respect for others and their ideas, sharing, taking and accepting responsibility, making rules and following them, negotiating mishaps, and accepting and adjusting behavior. Like all people, children need each day to be special and each moment to be savored as valuable and worth their time rather than always preparing for tomorrow. The best preparation for being a contributing citizen in society involves spending each moment in school as conscientious, caring citizens of our community.

Child-centered education and play are part of childhood (really any age) and do not need a program such as the Integrated Day to sanction them. All classrooms need play. The words of Rabindranath Tagore, the Indian poet who influenced William Butler Yeats and contributed to the Education Reform Movement in Bangladesh, ring true for my philosophy of teaching:

> What tortured me in my school days was the fact that the school had not the completeness of the world. It was a special arrangement for giving lessons. It could only be suitable for grownup people who were conscious of the special need of such places and therefore ready to accept their teaching at the cost of disassociation from life. But children are in love with life, and it is their first love. All its color and movement attract their eager attention. Are we quite sure of our wisdom in stifling this love?

The following pages offer what I think of as recipes for learning that contain my teaching experiences with young children and insights on ways to encourage play that powers children's learning. Teachers and parents can adapt my ideas for play to their own teaching or parenting style and the needs of their children. As Tagore said, " . . . children are in love with life . . . " When we genuinely like or love children, show respect for their dignity, and trust in their ability to learn, the magic of learning is shared. *The Power of Play and Learning* presents a pantry of ideas to envision children at play, play that is symbiotic with learning and working. Play is children's work, and it starts with an invitation to interact.

The Integrated Day teachers wrote "Assumptions Underlying the Integrated Day Program" for a handbook that was given to interested parents. The assumptions along with my teaching philosophy clearly communicate the foundational thinking of the program and my teaching.

My Teaching Philosophy

Each student is accepted as a learner.

*Education is achieved only when an individual has a
strong inherent desire to learn and
make sense of his or her environment.*

All people need success to prosper.

*Education should strive to maintain the individuality and
originality of the learner.*

*True learning is attained through
inquiry, discovery, and application.*

The individual develops through processes.

*Each learner perceives the learning process as related to
his or her own sense of reality.*

*An individual must be allowed to work according to
his or her own abilities and must
never be made to feel inferior to others.*

Play is a child's work.

The role of the teacher is as a facilitator and a guide.

*The learning environment must be compatible to reality and
expanded to meet the needs of the students.
It must be ever changing and not remain stagnant.*

Learning involves community.

*When students feel a sense of responsibility,
they grow to be caring, responsible adults.*

Assumptions Underlying the Integrated Day Program

1. A school, a classroom, should be a rich learning environment deliberately designed with much to explore and in which to become active. It should extend into the community and relate to the home. The teacher's role is to assess and guide the learning toward long-range objectives.

2. The developmental psychologist Erik Erikson calls the stage from ages five to twelve the Age of Industry. The child learns best when he is active, moving, communicating, sharing, tinkering, putting things together, taking things apart, manipulating concrete materials; in short using all his senses in activities that are real to him.

3. As an active learner, the child is the principal agent in her own development. She is innately curious about the world and initiates activity to explore and learn about it. Learning is something a child does; it is not something done to her.

4. Each child is unique in the way he learns. The best learning starts from the child's experiences and interests. To a child reality is a whole, a unity, not divided into separate subject areas and isolated skills. Play is a child's work. When a child initiates activity in which he gets involved, she or he is playing and working.

5. Over a period of time every child should learn important skills and principles such as the Three Rs. These are tools of our culture. Most children come to school wanting to learn them.

6. Children need to learn to live together. They need the chance to experiment socially as well as intellectually. They need adults who are dedicated to help them work through the solutions to their human problems as well as their academic ones.

7. Aesthetics are at the heart of a child's world. As Charles Silberman who wrote *Crisis in the Classroom* says, "Poetry, music, painting, dance, and other arts are not frills to be indulged in if there is time left over from the real education, they are the real education."

8. Assessment of a child's efforts and growth should be made on the basis of her individual learning. How one child compares to another is not crucial to the teacher's work, rather that each child have opportunities to employ her own powers in activities that have meaning. Mistakes are not failures. Evaluation must not be turned into judgment.

9. Childhood is a stage of life itself, to be enjoyed and savored, it is not something simply to passed through to adulthood.

Play Constructs Thinking in the Interactive Classroom

Play is often talked about as if it were a relief from serious learning.
But for children, play is serious learning.

—Fred Rogers

The language of play is flexible, yet children abide by strict rules they develop through iterations of play. In some ways, rules evolve implicitly and clearly to everyone playing. In other ways, rules develop to address conditions created by the game itself and the constraints of the play area. The language of play develops imagination, yet it is reality centered. The language of play manipulates, yet it compromises. Above all, ideas flourish in play, thereby challenging and stretching the mind, all while children (and adults) have fun.

Children discover their own truths as they construct meaning while playing. Piaget, a pioneer in understanding children's learning stages, believes the way children learn informs the meaning of play. Children become aware as they consciously react to their environment, a key to cognitive development.

Children form their perceptions from their need to know, thus enabling them to make sense of their environment at all levels of development: social, emotional, physical, spiritual, or individual. An ideal school environment nurtures children's drive to know rather than limits it by requiring children to sit still for an extended time, keeping quiet, or working on worksheet after worksheet. Learning is not a high-speed, one-way drive down a superhighway.

Children discover apparent truths or act on presumed possibilities, develop hypotheses, and test them. For example, dumping a container of sand makes it spread out. If a child pours sand from a higher distance, it spreads farther. Repeated sand play tests and refines understanding of the experience by constantly refining the hypothesis. While forming not only a concept for observed processes but also similar concepts, the process leads to understanding gravity, the motion of a pendulum, and spatial relationships. The sand experience becomes a hook to grasp future, more developed ideas.

Like sponges, children absorb knowledge from experiences in their environment.

Like sponges, children absorb knowledge from experiences in their environment. When a predicted outcome does not materialize, conflict occurs followed by further questioning of the prediction. The conflict forces the child to develop a new hypothesis and broaden the depth of knowledge used to base further revision. Children accept new information until they encounter a new conflict. The brain processes the new information and refines the old information. For ideal play and learning to take place, the environment must support and encourage the quest to construct a knowledge base.

Classroom or living space should say: *This is our safe, kind, magical room where we will learn about our world. We'll sing, listen, laugh, understand, play, and grow.*

The Shared Learning Environment

Structuring an environment for learning through play requires listening to the children's needs and together setting expectations and rules for social and academic order within the physical environment. Ownership of the environment is important. Not all children may have the same enthusiasm about a specific topic, but all children like to create. When children have control over their immediate world, their interest shows in their involved behavior, interactions with others, language usage, problem solving, and written responses. When sharing responsibility for the room with children, the teacher will find it natural to accept a higher noise level and provide opportunities for children to share learning, thereby fostering connections, solving problems, and generating new ideas. Everyone must work together to set standards for classroom safety and respect because each child shares the ownership of the environment that serves the individual's or the group's purpose.

The play environment says: *This is your place to wonder and seek answers and to use materials in order to see what they can do. All who share this learning environment show respect to each other. We need to take care of materials and cooperate because we share ownership.*

When we provide a cognitively stimulating environment and invite children's contributions to its making, children will interact with it

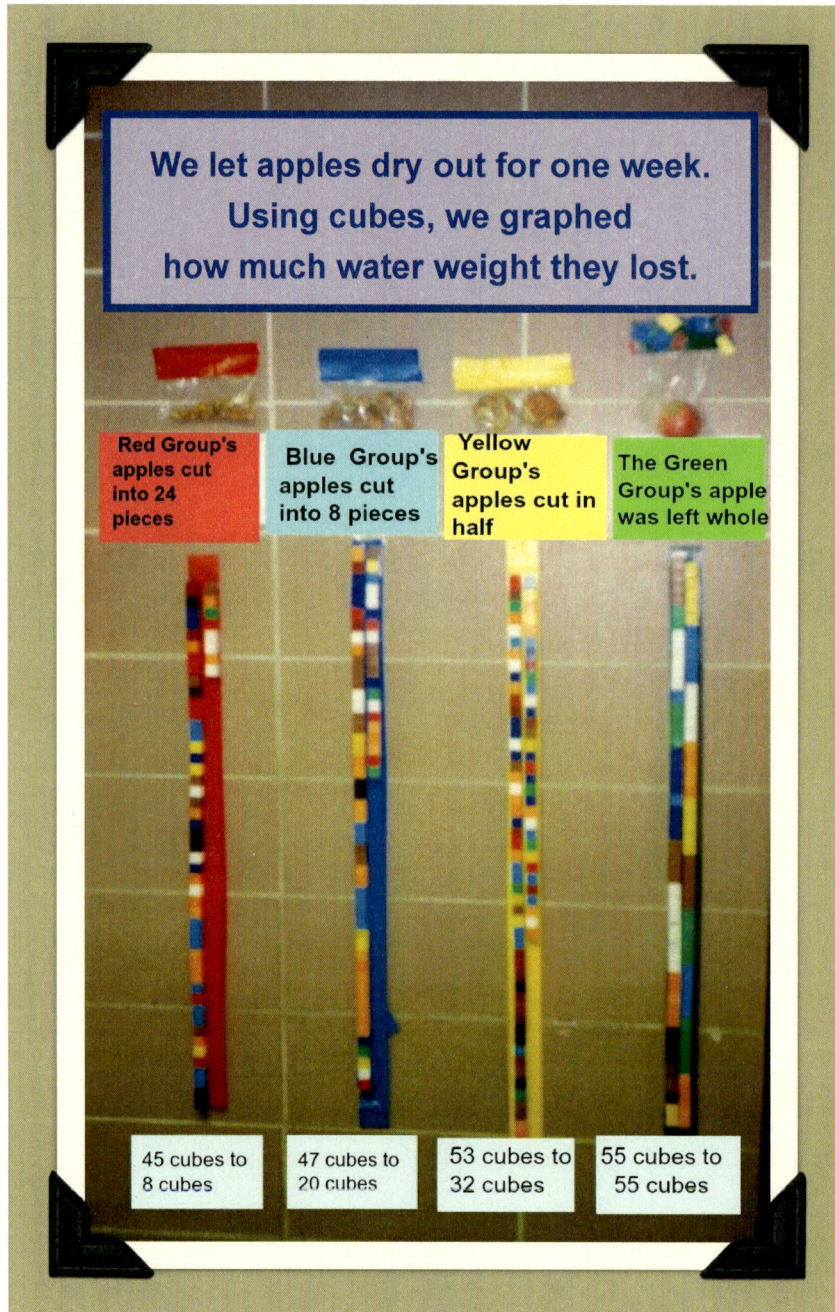

We let apples dry out for one week.
Using cubes, we graphed
how much water weight they lost.

Red Group's apples cut into 24 pieces

Blue Group's apples cut into 8 pieces

Yellow Group's apples cut in half

The Green Group's apple was left whole

45 cubes to 8 cubes

47 cubes to 20 cubes

53 cubes to 32 cubes

55 cubes to 55 cubes

*The chart, above, shows results after children measured and
compared the daily water loss of a whole apple,
an apple cut in half, and apples cut in pieces.
They snapped plastic Unifix cubes into line graphs to represent
units used to weigh the apple on a balance scale and
displayed graphs in the hallway.*

educationally, physically, emotionally, and spiritually through play. Such play embraces motivation, enthusiasm, effort, quality, and reflection. Through play, children masterfully build knowledge. As teachers, we can tap into that dynamo of energy and not have to work to engage the learners because they will be self-motivated to learn in an environment they have a stake in. Play is children's work in the learning environment they share. We adults observe, question, and listen. Our job is to watch their play and enhance it with developmentally appropriate problems and materials for learning.

An Inviting Space for Play

The best learning environment has space, equipment, and materials that say: *I am here for you to grow and learn. Care for me with kindness. Use me safely and creatively, and I will help you discover.* The space can be small or spacious, the equipment sparse or elaborate, and the materials few or plentiful. Early childhood teachers have always used ingenuity; they are masters of making do, begging, borrowing, asking parents and neighbors for household items, or asking other teachers to share supplies and materials.

The room must be inviting. A colleague stopped by my room because his children wondered about the room that produced such interesting murals, graphs, charts, and stories in the hallway. One child said, "Wow. They play all day." I was elated. The room said what I had hoped. The space in my room, filled with materials, said: *Come in and play. I am part of your world.* The room setup provides opportunities to learn not only from the materials but also from each person in the room, including me.

Places for Opportunities to Experiment and Learn Together

Thoughtful interaction is the attitude of play that maximizes the value of an experience. Each day, we must offer opportunities for thoughtful experiences and interactions that encourage inductive and deductive thinking. Together, children make new discoveries. They develop and test hypotheses. With social interaction, children validate and respect each other's ideas. They share the responsibility and care for themselves, materials,

Children share and listen to each other.

and equipment. Thoughtful interaction creates relevant communication of feelings, needs, and ideas to build authentic, shared experiences. As well, play allows children to move and encourages physical development.

Carefully chosen equipment and child-centered activities in clearly identified spaces create maximum opportunities for thoughtful interaction.

Play is natural and can be found throughout the animal kingdom as a way to teach young animals about survival in their environment. A mother cat encourages her kittens to play and learn about their surroundings. Giving them a stunned mouse to play with, the mother watches as the kittens practice their hunting and survival skills. She intrudes only to refocus their play to achieve the goal of teaching them to get food. Play gives each kitten a better chance to make judgments through experiences.

Effective teaching involves similar recursive strategies: providing materials, setting goals for learning, and observing the learning process. The teacher intervenes to

- call attention to a particular unsafe choice
- show kindness and offer accolades for specific work
- point out a particular discovery
- ask a question to further stretch thinking
- validate a particular insight demonstrated
- extend the student's thinking or knowledge base
- notice antisocial behavior
- call attention to time constraints
- offer clean up help if needed

Class discussions after play give children opportunities to describe and reflect on their discoveries. Providing time for discussion allows children to learn new ideas from others, enhancing their own play experience. While listening to the discussion, the teacher assesses the learning needs of each student for future planning.

Opportunities to play at school are opportunities to work and learn. Play at school is a child's work because it is not a diversion but rather a way of engaging in all facets of the child's mind, heart, and body. John Dewey, an American philosopher, psychologist, and educational reformer, whose ideas have been influential in education and social reform, argued that play is subjective. Dewey said play is pure foolishness without a connection to work, which he believed must be self-motivating in young children. Learning through play is intrinsic. Play is learning because it involves thinking, resolving questions, planning, meeting obstacles, changing premises, solving problems, and developing new questions, just as work does.

Dewey described play as a learning process that gains meaning as learning activities grow more challenging. Learning deepens in complexity as children apply greater attention to specific results they are achieving while problem solving or discovering through inquiry. As well, the children develop and deepen their shared value in their social setting. Play uses John Dewey's scientific method of learning as a means to achieve other learning goals. The child has an experience, draws conclusions, develops a hypothesis to test over time, and often draws a new conclusion. Just as in life, the process constantly changes. The teacher or parent must provide real-life experiences for the child to set goals for thinking.

An integrated multidisciplinary curriculum with tools to make and create learning activities or problems to solve provides children the optimal environment for social and intellectual engagement. Not only is it interpersonal social engagement but also intrapersonal. Such socio-cognitive interaction is play and work merged, resulting in effective, intrinsically motivated learning.

> *An integrated multidisciplinary curriculum with tools to make and create learning activities or problems to solve provides children the optimal environment . . .*

Classroom Essentials

Creating a room filled with appealing areas and accessible materials for children to think and explore is the most important ingredient. Children's interest span is often shorter for teacher-directed activities than for self-chosen activities.

The learning environment must include space for active body movement for games, rhythm bands, marching, dancing, and climbing. We often walked to the cafeteria if we needed a larger space for a play or performance. Ease of movement is essential for students to access materials, to clean work spaces, and to display projects.

Teachers can arrange tables allowing from two to four students at each, depending on whether they are working with pencil and paper, art materials, or reading and discussing. Classrooms need a large space for group meetings, discussions, and language arts activities and smaller spaces for pairs or small groups reading books, listening to music, or creating art projects. Since children are kinesthetic learners, all materials must be touchable and workable. Most children need help to keep materials in order. All materials should be clearly labeled and the setup of each area easy for children to straighten up. The following list shows the breadth of materials in spaces I created for a thoughtful classroom filled with interactions:

A Book Nook provides a place for reading or listening to high interest books and magazines. Cushions, pillows or beanbag chairs allow children to relax and enjoy reading. Thematic stories and activities from various children's magazines and books on the topic being studied fill containers. This collection includes science, social studies, and math-related materials in print and audio. For example, before our unit on rocks, I collected several books about rocks, recorded the text for listening, and highlighted where the recording started in the text. This allowed materials of higher reading level to be appreciated. I read slowly with emotion, so the children could easily follow the words. Today, many books are already on audio and can be accessed on the internet. However, the pace of the reading needs to be considered if the goal is for children to read and listen.

An Art Cart, a creative storage unit with student materials for art projects, may be on rolling wheels or stationary, but it must be near a table or an easel for easy access. I arranged the art cart neatly with various materials: scissors, different types and colors of paper, glue, trims, material scraps, yarn, stamps and stamp pads, stickers, clays, paints, and assorted novelty texture items such as buttons and jewels. The teacher can keep additional art materials, such as seasonal supplies, in a cabinet. Varying materials adds interest.

Reading partners enjoy reading together.

A Writing Center contains many materials. Mine had wall space to hold class-generated word lists and pictures of the current learning theme. There was a shelf area to hold supplies: magnetic boards, white boards, paper journals, writing pads, colored markers, pencils, crayons, chalkboards, materials for forming letters such as finger paint or shaving cream. Children were able to take these materials any place in the room to write. There were globes and maps used to identify geographical locations, names of land masses and oceans of the world.

An Area for Dramatic Play includes a table, sink, and other furniture. Children transformed this space into a doctor's office with stethoscopes and bandages, a Native American teepee furnished with baskets and fur rugs, a Pilgrim homestead with a weaving loom, Beatrix Potter's house when we fell in love with Peter Rabbit stories, or any habitat needed for dramatic play.

Children create a doctor's office in the area for dramatic play.

A Puppet Theater has a collection of characters to encourage students to model behaviors, tell fantasy tales, or retell stories.

A Science Area has many scientific objects to explore and manipulate in experiments. I put the area in my classroom next to a cabinet filled with collections of shells, rocks, buttons, magnets, or bread tags—any sortable items—for Choice Board time. I included magnifying glasses and colored lenses, eyedroppers, beakers, plastic tubes, funnels, different-sized containers for measuring, magnets, scoops, string, and kaleidoscopes for scientific discovery.

A Math Area contains math manipulatives available for easy retrieval during Choice Board time. The children especially liked using Cuisenaire

In the science area, a student discovers the power of magnetism.

In the math area, two students measure and take notes.

rods or pattern blocks to design three-dimensional colored pictures. We had playing cards, dice, math games, Geoboards, and problem boards for extra fact practice.

A Computer Area hosts online reading, writing, math games, geography and current events. I included this area on the Choice Board as a station for class study or individual projects.

A Listening Center includes listening and recording devices: CD players, electronic music players, and electronic tablets with headphones and microphones. Students listened to stories and music or recorded their reading.

A Two-Sided Large Easel is big enough for up to three children to paint or draw on one side. I often used the other side as a big-book easel

Children create at a two-sided easel.

for reading, math graphing with stamps, and creating storyboards for plot sequences or puppet shows, pictorial scripts, or writing practice.

A Building Area stacked with blocks, Legos, and large-sized cardboard blocks encourages dramatic play. I included people figures of many ethnicities, furniture, signs, cars, gas pumps, and other building and dramatic play materials.

The Choice Board stays in an accessible place where students can choose their learning activities. The teacher establishes how many choices,

Wooden blocks allow imaginative play.

depending on need. Students can work from a Learning Contract and choose designated activities over time.

A Sandbox Area includes a large container filled with sand, cornmeal or rice and tools used to dig, sift, measure, build, and weigh.

A Water Table or a plastic bin with various sizes of containers and a waterwheel offers opportunities for measuring, pouring, experimenting, and exploring. It is advisable to keep sand and water separate and provide opportunities to mix them for specific scientific inquiry of different properties of matter.

A Map Area has a good supply of old maps. The middle school or high school often has old ones. Old, larger wall maps make great floor maps, too. Though countries may have changed since publication of an old map, oceans and land masses remain the same. Maps familiarize children with direction.

We played many games using the maps. For example: Throw a beanbag at the same time announcing an ocean. If the bag lands on the named ocean, the player gets another turn. If missed, the name of the place the bag landed is named. All players can help each other. When all can name the oceans, go on to naming the countries. On one map we outlined journeys of Marco Polo and other sea explorers. We invented a math game to follow their paths. They learned much more than the names of the continents because I asked about explorers. I showed them how to look up the information the old-fashioned way, using an encyclopedia in book form.

Children find oceans and countries while examining a floor map.

A Rug Area with rug squares allows the whole class to come together.

A Chart Stand houses graphs, calendar, songs, or poems.

A Climbing Structure with ladders leading to an upper level and an open space below can occupy a central spot in the classroom. Play on the climber strengthens large muscles and upper body. In my classroom, the climber from time to time became a store, ship, aquarium, or another theme-related space.

Book Making starts at the beginning of each school year. I sent a letter to parents about ways to help in the classroom or at home. One of the requests was for sewn or stapled booklets to be made. When parents checked that particular item, I sent directions and some white and colored copy paper. I sent a long arm stapler if the parent didn't want to sew. One resourceful parent handstitched a large running stitch with yarn and tied bows. We used booklets for recording math, science, and language arts. I liked to have extras for children to use to make books during Choice Time.

At the beginning of the year, I also sent a request letter home a encouraging parents to send in lace and anything extra that could be useful. For example, one parent sent in round facial cleansing pads that children transformed into puppet faces.

Directions for Booklets

Take four sheets of white paper and one sheet of colored paper; fold them exactly in half the wide way. Open the paper and stitch down the center with the widest stitch possible. Return completed books to the classroom.

Sturdy books with cardboard can also be made. I covered them with wallpaper and then clear contact paper. I used heavy tape for the binding. Then we glued the sewn books in them.

Asking Parents for "Beautiful Junk"

Dear Parents,

We would like you to save some "beautiful junk" for our ongoing art and math projects. The following is a partial list, but any small object or larger building material would also be useful. Do let me know, however, if you have large building materials available. I may want you to store them until a project comes up for their use. Please save and send in with your child any of the following throughout the year:

Toothpicks

Buttons

Rice

Clean, old socks

Old towels - we spill often

Old calendars

Assorted jewelry

Doll clothes

Old T-shirts

Trims: lace, rickrack, eyes, etc.

Styrofoam trays

Newspapers

Shoeboxes (save one at home)

Plastic containers—all sizes

Materials to make costumes

Detergent/spray can tops

Wood scraps - for gluing and hammering

Egg cartons

Cardboard tubes

Flattened cereal boxes (We use the cardboard for books or art projects at Choice Board time.)

Milk cartons

String or shoelaces

This week we are studying balancing and need an approximately three-inch-by-ten-inch pegboard.

Please have your child bring the item(s) in and put them on our recycle bookshelf. Children will have a chance to show what they brought in at share time. Thank you for your help.

Sincerely,
MaryJane Devlin

Sandbox Play and Exploration

Play is the highest form of research.

—Albert Einstein

Many opportunities develop thoughtful interaction within the school day. One such versatile learning opportunity is what happens when children use the sandbox. Sandbox play is filled with endless learning possibilities to further concepts in math, science, art, and writing. Children may also experience thematic units and learn about social interactions during sandbox play.

Teachers who feel pressured to cover too much curriculum may hesitate to include a sandbox. Yet, sandbox play is an asset, not a liability. Although children can be messy, they will accept the responsibility to clean up the area.

> *. . . through playing with sand, children develop their understanding of the scientific concept of matter and the many forms it takes as well as what it can do.*

I have heard teachers argue that dumping sand all over the place is not accomplishing anything. However, through playing with sand, children develop their understanding of the scientific concept of matter and the many forms it takes as well as what it can do.

A sandbox filled with real sand is vital and necessary to all children's learning. In a sandbox, young children pour sand repeatedly. They vary amounts, use different containers, and master self-control while experimenting with sand. Sand play is high-level thinking and provides hooks in children's brains, vital connections for future learning.

Today, children find themselves hurried to complete and assimilate more data without time to make connections through real life experiences. Repeated use of actual matter such as sand, develops children's intrinsic logic. They sort and further understand properties of the earth, weight, texture, feel, and volume. They develop a rich background for meaning along with physical and mental skills needed to respect sand. They not only master controlling it but also controlling themselves.

Children working in a sandbox develop considerable social interactive skills, including character development, social values, identifying appropriate and inappropriate behavior, and language skills to convey understanding through spoken and unspoken communication as they work alongside peers. Teachers can find many ways to capitalize on individual and group learning possibilities when children play in the sandbox.

If two or three play in the sandbox, they must care about others for safety and enjoyment. Children learn responsibility, rules of order, kindness, and respect while using the material, and in the end, they sweep up the sand for another day. When they choose to play in the sandbox, they accept community responsibilities and the consequences of inappropriate use. The teacher expects each child to use the material appropriately or the sandbox choice will not be an option for a given child during Choice Board time.

Most curricular and thematic projects can incorporate the sandbox for added enrichment. When a filled sandbox is readily available, the children think of more uses for the material.

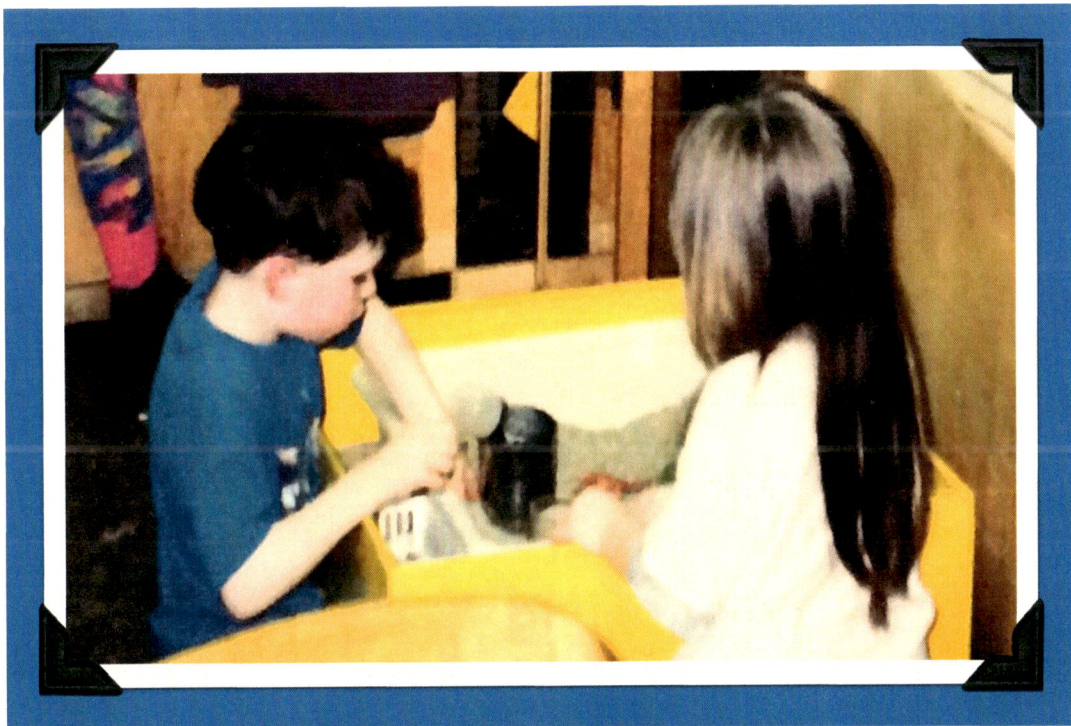

A sandbox provides space for creative play.

With a waterwheel, children learn about
gravity, flow, and the potential power of water.

Responsibility for Sand and Self

Inviting children to be responsible for their own learning, I asked them to suggest other materials for the sandbox. Together we came up with rice, beans, coffee beans, and cornmeal to fill the sand table. We used rocks, shells, water, clay, buttons, washers, and found materials for learning activities.

I set guidelines for use of specialty equipment requiring more control such as a sand wheel or waterwheel. Closer supervision and modeling how to use certain materials and equipment help students eventually take ownership. Discussion about the need for special care of a material opens awareness and often provides enough information to highlight the necessity for care.

When teachers encourage children to have input into decisions about their learning with provision for reflection and sharing the value of learning choices, children own their learning and make good choices. Teachers must hold high expectations for appropriate behavior and respect for choices. Of course, the teacher implements consequences for poor choices once children understand them.

Play in the sandbox leads to more confident lifelong learners, and young children who play in sandboxes will be on the road toward achieving their fullest potential.

Sand for Writing

After reading *Sylvester and the Magic Pebble* by William Steig, each student found a magic stone in the sandbox. They planned and wrote stories about their stones using a storyboard. Their stories included introductions describing setting and characters. They wrote about where, when, and how they found the stone and what happened. Kindergarteners drew pictures first on the storyboard and then told stories orally. Students were encouraged to use inventive spelling for writing a few letters or longer strings of words or sentences. Later, everyone had an opportunity to dictate or read his or her story to a parent volunteer. Children love to tell stories, especially when stories involve magic.

When evaluating writing, I asked students, "What is something you are proud of in your story?"

One child stated, "My best writing came out of the sandbox." He found his special stone there. He set his story in a park by a winding stream, where his special stone was hiding something. The writing held some excitement because he included an intriguing question: What was hiding under the special stone? The stone hid gold, which made him very lucky and rich.

Sand for Art

Sand Paint: Sprinkle colored sand on paths of glue. Use for murals, dioramas, and artifacts. (Sand paint recipe: mix ground colored chalk or powdered tempera paint with fine sand.)

Sand Glue: Add colored sand to glue as an alternative to provide texture to a picture. Use sand-glue paint with stenciled letters or numerals. Laminating bookmarks and having students paint on them with glue sand makes a fun activity that results in everyone having a bookmark. Paint using sand glue on Play-Doh, clay, or cardboard items for texture.

Molds: Use sand to make a paperweight mold for filling with liquid Plaster of Paris. Arrange objects such as shells and bits of other materials before pouring the plaster. Glue objects on the resulting paperweight as well.

Musical Instruments: Fill and cover containers or paper towel tubes with sand, then shake.

Sand for Math, Science, and Social Studies

Bury metal or other objects (such as shells, special stones, necklace materials, or theme artifacts)

Replace digging tools with magnets

Include toy animals and structures for constructing habitats

Include real coins (play money costs more)

Count the number or value of coins to bury in the sand. Predict how much money will come from one scoop. Finding and sorting similar coins and dissimilar coins or counting a mixture provides a fun way to learn about money values and adding. Record and graph findings as a class.

Student Choice

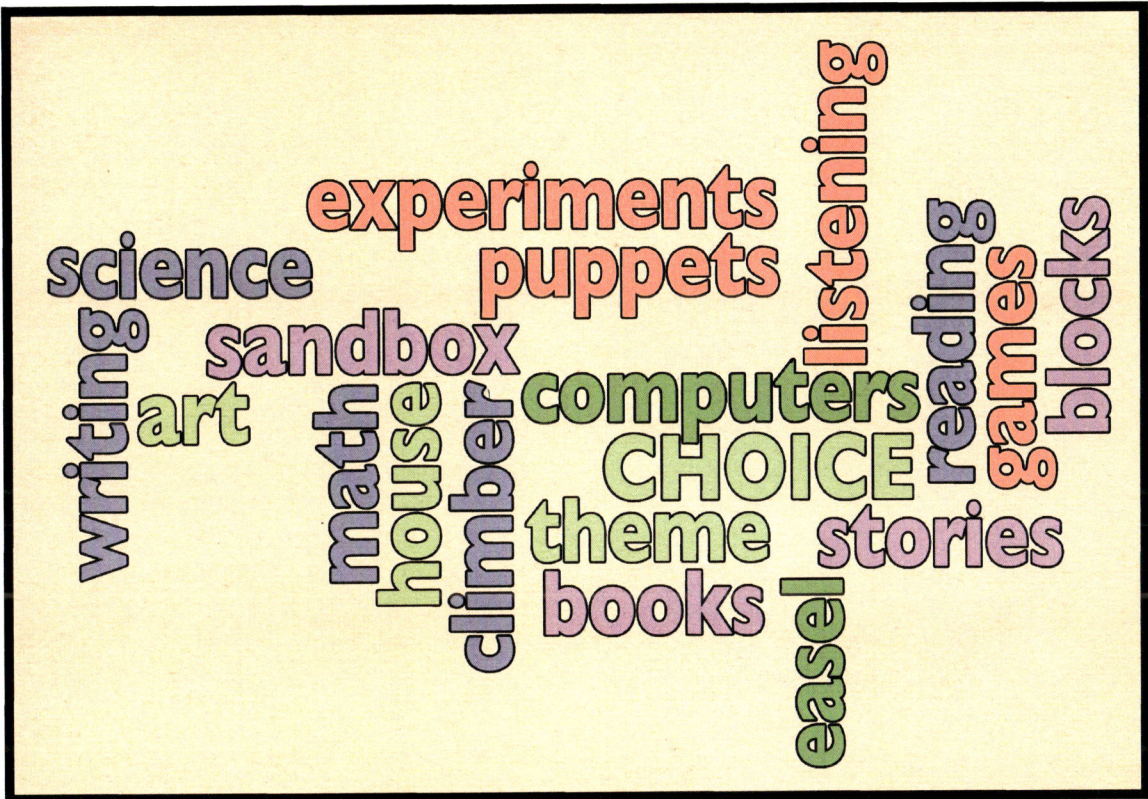

You are asking me questions, and I hear you.
I answer that I cannot answer you.
You must find out for yourself.

—Walt Whitman

Children learn more than half of what they will ever know before they reach the age of five by trying to make sense of their world. Often in school, adults tell children where they should be, what they need to know, the method by which they will learn, and in what order to do tasks. Often, adults delineate the timelines for learning and products. Such attributes of learning are specified from the beginning of school and continue for the rest of their school lives. We can change the model and must change the model by listening to children's voices. We can expand their vision and stimulate their environment with challenges so they can become involved and invested from the start. With that shared ownership and a learning environment set up for play and thoughtful interactions, student choice is important to play and learning.

We act or react to every stimulus we perceive. To enable children to make wise choices, we can teach them how to be aware of and in control of their choices. One of the most important skills for living and learning involves acknowledging every choice has a consequence. As teachers, we work to make children aware of their power to choose, as well as consequences of choices they make. It is important to give choices to children early on so they will become responsible learners. When children are having fun and feel interested and engaged in what they are doing, learning is taking place. Choice is a vehicle for that learning.

> *To enable children to make wise choices, we can teach them how to be aware of and in control of their choices.*

We make most of our choices as learned responses to daily life and often don't give the process another thought. Perhaps without realizing it, choices in our life build our strong and weak character traits, our value systems, our attitudes, and our special gifts. Our children need to live in an environment of choice to learn from the choices they make. From birth, children develop perceptions and values. They bring their perceptions and values to the classroom.

Young people develop character as they make sense of their world, which can be hectic and overpowering. Parents and teachers are partners by talking about morality and truth with our young people to help them grow and mature. Schools and home need to be partners when providing choice in their environments and to remember interaction comes alongside that choice. Schools often send a message to families to read with their children. However, the environment at school can offer fewer challenges than at home where decisions are made by an industry such as the media, which has an ever-increasing presence in our lives and, therefore, in the interactions of our students.

Messages from television influence how children conceptualize reality. Although much of what children see or hear on television has no truth, children watching shows may perceive them as true. They form attitudes about life accepted as the norm as portrayed by television characters. Television often shows stereotyped women as oversexed and ridiculing the other sex and stereotyped men as violent and uncaring, rudely or sarcastically demeaning each other. News programs bombard children with war, crime, and frightful events around the globe.

Even if parents block movies and adult material on television from their children, movie previews or commercials during programs depict adults drinking alcohol, gambling, or being goofy. Children can view from eight to ten minutes of commercial time during a thirty-minute program. Therefore, it is important to talk to our children so they understand how television shows are funded with commercial ads in hopes we will buy products. Just as adults react to products the commercial giants hope we will buy, children react the same way to toy commercials. Talking with children about what they view and hear on television demonstrates to them that, as consumers, we must take responsibility for questioning the media. It shows children they must make choices by asking "Why?"

If children come to school having had interactions about what they have viewed in the media, they have rehearsed some critical thinking that will inform their choices and discussions with their peers. Although addressing media may seem a bit of a side road to play, it is a thread of experience children may bring to their learning and interactions. It is something we adults in their lives need to monitor closely for its value in their development. A classroom environment that allows for choice and play allows children to make sense of competing messages and develop shared core values with their learning community.

More importantly, we must recognize and value the responsibility of personal choice, beginning during childhood. Teachers must encourage children to take responsibility for their actions, just as teachers must take responsibility for their own actions. That doesn't mean teachers let children do anything they would like or whenever they would like. As adults, we can (and should) control options for choice. Children appreciate limits. They structure their own play, generate rules for play, and design problems within a theme through dramatic play, construction play, material play, creative play, and exercise play.

Experiencing choice in school encourages more opportunities for being thoughtful decision-makers outside of school. As children experience making more choices, their thought process will include whether the choice will be harmful, and they will begin to consider potential consequences of a choice before making it.

Play and the Daily Choice Board

Of all techniques I used in my teaching repertoire, the Choice Board is by far the best. The Choice Board, a place where students may select the activity they would like to do, displays evolving academic, physical, artistic, and dramatic exploration choices as well as other thematic areas of interest. The use of a Choice Board solves many problems such as turn taking, the number of children in a learning area, classroom management, and meeting the many needs of individual learners. I made Choice Board a daily activity, even if I had to curtail the length of time allowed for the activity, because each student's awareness and practice of personal choice is an important lesson that must be taught and respected.

Creating a Choice Board

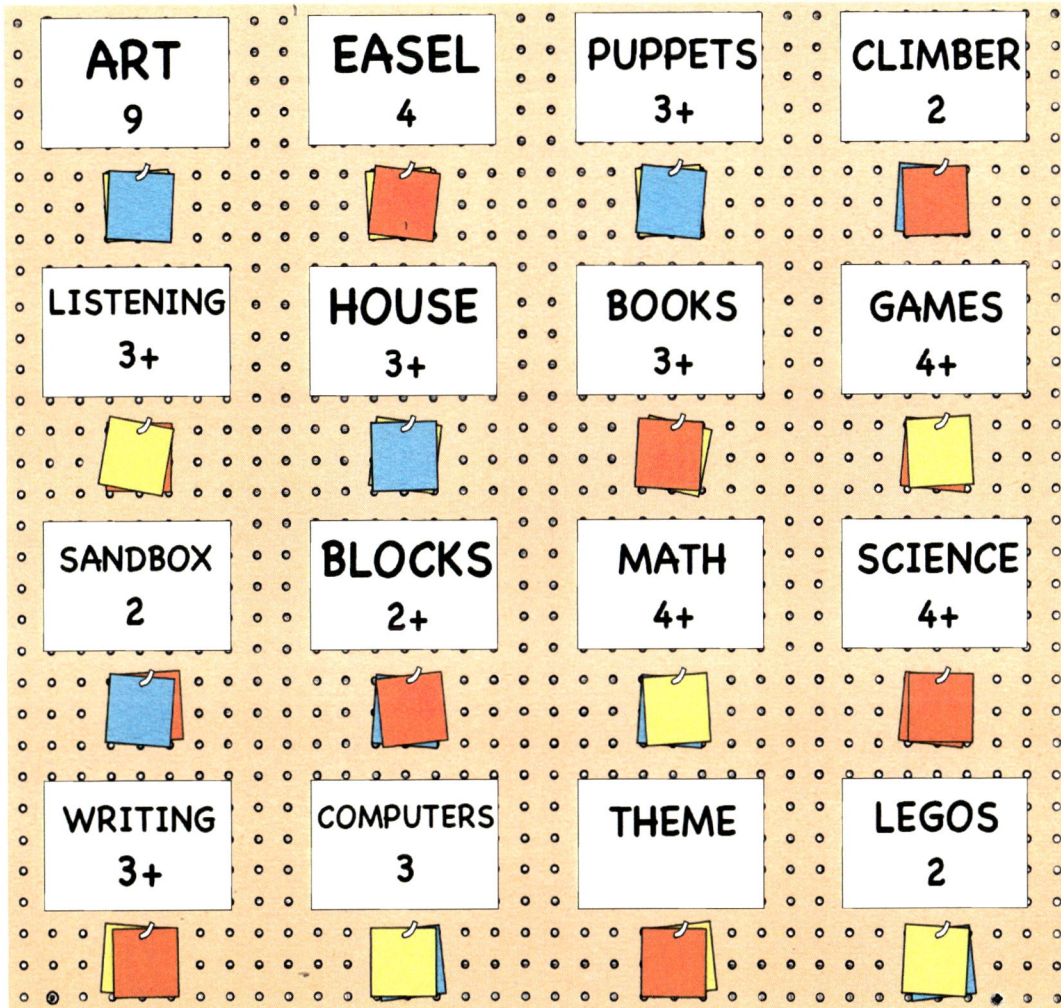

ART 9	EASEL 4	PUPPETS 3+	CLIMBER 2
LISTENING 3+	HOUSE 3+	BOOKS 3+	GAMES 4+
SANDBOX 2	BLOCKS 2+	MATH 4+	SCIENCE 4+
WRITING 3+	COMPUTERS 3	THEME	LEGOS 2

A Choice Board provides students options for activities.

Our Choice Board was a piece of painted pegboard (any board with hooks or pockets will do). I made mine three feet by four feet, but it could even be larger. It was divided into between twelve and sixteen sections. I secured choice title cards to the board after I copied the cards. The Choice

Board included theme choice with changing activities. There was a hook or hooks below the choice title card for students to place their name cards. I used the title cards to play games to familiarize children with their choices: lotto, matching or bingo games, or a station game.

Children moved around to different areas. The board displayed all potential areas of interest. During the day, students had time to experience play activities, arts, and academics. The board included laminated card stock squares, each with the name of an activity, the number of children who may play there, and a hook for students to hang their name cards.

All of the learning areas had one hook that could accommodate up to four students, except the Art area, because so many wanted to choose that area. The Art area offered plenty of space, supplies, and activities for everyone. It could have as many as twelve activities to choose from on a given day.

Keeping copies of the choice cards visible in the group meeting area helped students think about their learning choices. Students worked in different centers on different activities. For example, for our Native American unit, one choice for students was to make beads from clay. For our Coming-to-America unit, students could choose to make ships from milk cartons.

Launching and Managing the Choice Board

The easiest method I found for managing Choice Board sign-up was to make Choice Board student name cards from three different laminated colored card stocks. I cut the cards two and a half by three inches and punched a hole in the top of each card for ease in putting on a hook. I was sure to make extra cards because some get lost throughout the year, and it helps to have extras that you can easily access. I had the extras on three hooks, sorted by color.

For Choice Board sign-up, each child received a name card in one of three colors assigned to create groups. I rotated colors each week so each group had a turn being able to choose first. Name cards had other uses, for example, for classroom jobs. Children in a chosen color group would be

Children choose activities from the Choice Board at right.

responsible for calendar, emptying the pencil sharpener, passing out papers, or taking lunch money to the office. The student in charge of the calendar started the day. I also used color-coded groups to help establish and manage routines, stations, and daily themes.

Getting the children started on an activity might occur in different ways. I liked to sing the children's names. For example I would sing, "Joey came to school today; Joey came to school today, just to play." Singing got the children's attention and made each child feel special. The first child I sang to would publicly choose and announce what he or she wanted to play and put the card on the corresponding hook. Then the next person of the color group would go. After a time, once they knew the routine and recognized their written names, I would lay name cards out on a table for them to find independently.

A great deal of time must be spent modeling the play options. Through modeling, children become familiar with how to play in each area as new activities and games are added. Once children know the routine and how to manage their options, the Choice Board becomes one of the most important features in planning a day with endless learning possibilities.

Transitions

The entire day, including transitions, should have a child's perspective in mind. Transitions can become a challenge for many children and teachers alike. Although Choice Board relies on self-responsibility, it also relies on the reality of children who are doing different activities unexpectedly being asked to transition. I sang my way through transitions. Once children heard me sing, "Come to a meeting, come to a meeting, come to a meeting, and come right now," they changed course and walked to the meeting area on cue whenever and wherever they were, including Choice Board time. I set up this protocol from the beginning of the year, so they knew the expectation. It was important they respond at once in case of an emergency. Setting up expectations from Day 1 sets the tone for the year.

Choice Board is perfect for a preschool, kindergarten, or vertically grouped K-1. A modified version would be possible in the upper grades as an Independent Study Board and include student-generated options for academic studies.

Student Choice and Teacher Choice

Setting a specific time for children to use the Choice Board is important. The Choice Board may be used at other times during the day including at Teacher Choice times, when the teacher assigns individuals or small groups a specific skill or needed practice.

Students respect the teacher's option because they like the friendly Choice Board. Often children express reluctance about trying a difficult, unfamiliar task. When directed to such a learning area, they have practice trying something new and working toward mastery.

As children assume responsibility for their choices, teachers must encourage them to make simple choices within their developmental range to build confidence. Offering choice to children is a step toward becoming a responsible adult.

During Teacher Choice time, I used the Choice Board to provide extra challenge, individualize stations, and encourage extra practice by putting a child's name card on a particular activity. Therefore, I could assign a group of children together who would benefit from an activity, perhaps in the listening center or in the writing center, where I would join the learning activity to model for them, guide them, or have a conference.

If students were allowed free choice all the time, they might not choose more challenging learning opportunities for fear of failure. To keep track of learning activities they completed, I had them mark a chart that listed all of the choices. This allowed me to provide balanced choices during Teacher Choice time. All curriculum areas need formal skill practice time throughout the day. In my classroom reading, writing, math, blocks, music, and other activities were offered all day.

When I observed students who needed more time, further modeling, or re-teaching of a concept, I organized it during Teacher Choice time to provide intervention for personalized learning. I presented mini-lessons as both individual and group activities. Opportunities for quiet time balanced noisier, more movement-generated activities. Choice Board offered ample time for direct instruction in specific skill areas while being child-centered with time to play.

Productive negotiating is not always easy for the ego-centered young child and sometimes can be unsuccessful. Building trust means that children learn to accept failure as part of learning, while realizing they can revise expectations. Henry Ford said, "Failure is the opportunity to begin again, more intelligently." Trusting relationships allow children to be vulnerable, so they can learn from failures. Children bounce back and set new, revised goals, which is part of living in a complex world. Young children become masters at this. *Build trust in yourself and each other* offers a pervasive message in the classroom learning environment.

Children loved signing up at the Choice Board and their time spent doing its learning activities. Before learning about an integrated approach, I had always offered free Choice Board time for play but asked everyone to do the same work at the same time during content area times. I found some students processed and learned quickly while others needed more time. The students who were finished would get bored and wanted to know what was next. In an integrated learning environment, options are readily available, and learning is ongoing. It was exciting to watch and be part of. When I asked at the end of each year what they liked best about class, being able to choose what to play was their favorite subject in school.

As a teacher, I loved Choice Board, too, because it provided authentic learning, engagement, and fun. Choice Board time brings learning opportunities for children to build trust and relationships while working together toward learning objectives and competencies. Through play, children more readily accept differences in others' ideas and cultures. They reach meaningful understanding as they construct knowledge and self-confidence in their competence and ability to try again.

The Choice Board's Flexible Options

Since each area had its own metal hook on the Choice Board, I could easily remove a hook for any activity that would not be an option for a given day. I removed a particular hook when other school-day tasks needed to be addressed or accomplished or when a consequence for inappropriate behavior eliminated using a particular material or equipment. Being able to remove choices served as an essential tool for classroom management. I also removed choices if something simply wasn't in place to offer a particular choice. For example, if the clay was not ready, the clay card was removed and not an option.

Student name cards rested on hooks on the right side of the Choice Board. Some choice cards had a plus sign (+) that meant the activity had room for another student. A child could ask to be added to the area. The plus sign allowed me to decide if adding another child was a good idea. I considered space, time, and needs of individuals when I made my decision. If I approved, the child was directed to ask the playing children if he or she could play.

Most children already playing in an activity would include new children and say, "Sure." I imagined they saw it as a compliment and appreciated having the choice. If children responded "No" to the child who wanted to join, the child learned not to take the children's negative decision as a personal rejection but rather that it wasn't a good time to join the activity.

Children had the option to change activities during Choice Board time by moving their name card to another hook, but they had to clean up before they went to another area unless their cleaning up would spoil the play of others, as in the house or blocks. At the end of playtime, children cleaned their area and helped others put our room back in order.

Thematic Studies Using the Choice Board

The Choice Board can be set up for any unit of study. For example, when we studied the Mohegan-Pequot Native Americans, I collected Native American poetry and stories to look at or listen to as a Choice Board's Listening Center card. I added activities for math games for the Math choice card using colored stones. For the House choice card, I had them crush acorns to make real flour, and for Art choice card, I asked children to assume the identity of a Native American hunting fowl. Then, they could choose to make a bow and arrow or paper-bag vest.

One November, while studying Coming to America, the students pretended to be children on the *Mayflower* and transformed our child climber into the hold of the ship. The ship was designed with a bow mathematically engineered first with blocks and later made of wood (with a little help from my husband). The ship had a stern, a mast, and a very large sail. During Choice Board time, children painted props and added their own necessities. There was a captain, an anchor, and a handmade compass so they would not get lost on the vast Atlantic Ocean. Children wrote their own scripts based on what they had learned. Adults might struggle if confined for thirty minutes in the little closed

Imaginatively, children turn the classroom climber into the Mayflower *with costumes and props.*

space of a climber, but the children had no problem. They were sailors doing their jobs or Pilgrim parents taking care of their children, who were playing or sleeping. They realized the Pilgrim children they emulated had to be polite on their walks on the stern and often had to stay below deck for long periods of time. As Pilgrim children, they played cat's cradle, read books, created lessons on a chalkboard, and sang to crying babies. I don't remember anyone quitting the game before playtime ended or the ship landed.

Here were active five- and six-year-olds who might wiggle and squirm trying to sit still for a five-minute lesson. How did they do it? They wanted to be on the *Mayflower*, demonstrating their understanding of what Pilgrims went through on their way to America. They showed their ability to stay on task, concentrate, and be resourceful while problem solving. They articulated appropriate content vocabulary in their conversations, their understanding of the needs of people during Early America, and their creativity through play.

Student Self-Evaluation of Learning

The children in my class studied in an atmosphere of play and made decisions about their learning. I provided time for students to share and reflect, which allowed them to validate their learning during Choice Board time. Evaluation meetings addressed problems. Children evaluated their learning in various ways from writing and sketching to orally sharing their assessment of their learning. Since Choice Board time was a valued learning opportunity, it also included student self-evaluation of learning.

I tried to capitalize on reflection time by varying the methods I used. Reflection was as simple as asking the students at the end of the day: "What was your best learning today?"

My favorite reflection method incorporated a cooperative note-taking technique. In this technique, three or four children playing in an area worked together. One folded a paper in fourths and put a child's initial in each corner. The children then proceeded to tell each other what they had learned, and the child chosen as a recorder drew a simple picture or wrote a few words that helped him or her remember what was said in order to share later with the class.

The recorder then shared the group's reflection with the larger group by saying, for example, "Amy likes when the puppet sang." The recorder then shared for all three or four children of the group. The process took from five to fifteen minutes, and the benefits were fantastic. All of the children listened politely and got the main idea of what was shared. They also learned a valuable note-taking technique. The recorder and note-taker roles changed each time, so all students got a chance to report out—since children love to show and tell.

A benefit of a group reflection is that, once the teacher introduces reflecting on a real play situation, there develops a cooperative group technique integral in an active class. Putting the ownership on the students provides growth in their individual efficiency, cohesiveness working with a group, and learning to respect all ideas shared. Cooperative group sharing allows children to work together to solve problems in math, share reading and responding in pairs, plan for Choice Board time, solve group behavioral issues, and even write in groups. I found that cultivating children's ability to listen to each other, record pertinent facts, and best utilize time is well worth the effort to teach them how to be reflective thinkers, an important life skill.

Play is the rehearsal of life's meaning, the crystallization of knowing, understanding, creating, and being. It is ever changing, adapting, reflective, and exciting. "Please, give us time to play," our children are pleading. "Please, give us time to be curious, to explore, and to make mistakes." Play turns inquiring minds into critical thinkers, designers, and creators.

> *Play is the rehearsal of life's meaning, the crystallization of knowing, understanding, creating, and being. It is ever changing, adapting, reflective, and exciting.*

The Learning Web

Life must be lived as play.

—Plato

Just as the students and I shared ownership with the daily Choice Board, we also shared ownership of the Learning Web, which served as a guide for thematic study. Creating the Learning Web provided time for students to choose what they wanted to learn. They helped by coming up with ideas for activities to achieve learning goals as well as ideas for a culminating activity to synthesize and share their learning. Our Sea Life Web is an example of one Learning Web unit of study that I will explore in more detail in a later chapter, "Sea Life: A Sample Thematic Unit."

Teachers can orchestrate changes to, additions to, or deletions from the Learning Web at any time. For instance, while working on Learning Web activities, if children showed particular interest in or would benefit from extended learning on one phase of the Learning Web, I made it happen by adding to the Learning Web. I never found a group who wasn't enthusiastic about planning a rich play theme or telling me all they knew about a topic to put into the Learning Web.

Planning and integrating core subjects to cover curriculum expectations together as a class motivates students because their voices are heard and their ideas considered. The children and I mapped out an in-depth Learning Web that helped us learn about a required topic of study. The students willingly focused and accepted learning in various modes. I found that a thematic approach allowed me to cover more academic and content areas than a traditional, compartmentalized approach.

Use of the Learning Web is the beginning of thematic play. It enables the teacher to plan for both right-brained and left-brained learning styles in most activities and allows the children to extend modalities by stretching less used parts of the brain. In this chapter, I mention subject areas only to highlight possibilities, but in the classroom I presented them simultaneously in an interwoven, interdisciplinary manner, not separated.

With curricular objectives always in mind, I gathered the class for a "What-do-we-want-to-learn?" Learning Web meeting. We began by brain-storming, considering each question a child or the teacher raised about the topic. The Learning Web brainstorming is essential to engage students and motivate them to want to learn more. I wrote the ideas directly on chart paper, which became our rough draft Learning Web. I assessed student interest by the group's prior knowledge and their enthusiasm during prior learning. I also evaluated how practical it would be to implement their suggestions and if there were special interest topics for individualized learning.

My role during creation of the Learning Web was to facilitate inquiry, ask questions about elements of learning, gather materials, and guide thinking to connect the web to past learning. During the process, I made sure our plans addressed core curriculum requirements. I mapped out play activities and determined how we would evaluate learning. Children were active in evaluating what they had learned.

For each part of the Learning Web, the learning focus changes. During creative arts play, children may be challenged to work on a math or science problem or they might develop an artistic or social need while at the same time practicing important skills such as writing numerals or letters. Yet, the activity presents simply as drawing and, therefore, engaging. I used creative arts as integral in weaving materials to merge information. For example, depending on what material is used, the experience of an activity and focus of the web changed. Children could draw with all kinds of enriching creative options from crayons, paint, and pencils to shaving cream. Any play venue builds in creativity.

We included on our Learning Web project ideas that helped answer questions through math, science, language arts, social studies, and art. Projects and learning interrelated with play capitalize on more than one subject at a time. Additionally, we listed ways to change our classroom environment—our space—so we could live in it while studying the particular topic or play themes. For example, we might change the climber to a rainforest or the house area into a doctor's office.

We did not complete the Learning Web in one day because it was an evolving Learning Web, meaning we updated and revised over several days.

Students in first grade developed skeletal thematic Learning Webs in their morning session of an all-day, first-grade program, and kindergarteners added to it when they came in the afternoon, each group learning from the other. Since kindergarteners looped with me a second year as first graders, they then enjoyed the opportunity to lead the learning.

Once we completed the thematic Learning Web, it became the foundation for Choice Board activities. The theme card on the Choice Board provided learning explorations relating to the theme.

Children can articulate what they are curious to know. I entered into this "wonder-about" area, too, and suggested curricula to address their needs. If an area was weak in a thematic idea, I asked, "What could we do in math?" The children then came up with creative, inventive ideas in subject areas not only with questions but also with ways to do the activities. By planning with the children, I integrated study and play explorations connected to their choices.

Since the Learning Web spanned a month of our curriculum for projects that included play while capitalizing on learning in all content areas, the next step of planning and preparation proved the most time consuming. I needed to gather props and transform the classroom, filling it with thematic materials.

There is no sugarcoating the amount of time involved in planning and preparing this type of learning environment. I spent hours scouring library shelves for stories and informational books to enrich learning. At home, I collected real artifacts to bring in to share. I arranged guest speakers and field trips.

As I assessed what materials we would need, I sent home a letter to parents explaining our new theme and time frame. In the letter, I offered ways they could help: gather books, come in and share experiences, or send in needed items. Parents are an invaluable resource. Their children's enthusiasm became contagious. Ensuring differentiated instruction and valuable learning experiences takes time. The thematic integrated approach is worth the effort.

Learning Web Culminating Activity

A culmination activity can be chosen while the Learning Web is in progress. The idea is to provide a chance for the children to shine. We did not use multiple-choice or fill-in-the-blank tests but rather performance-based demonstration of mastery. Children demonstrated understanding in many ways. At least once a year, students produced a book individually and one as a class. Possible publications included a book of research, poetry, or a play. We organized a special event to share the works with an audience. Each student shared poems or a story during an author's chair evening. We wrote plays and puppet shows and invited other classes, parents, and friends to come.

> *We did not use multiple-choice or fill-in-the-blank tests but rather performance-based demonstration of mastery.*

Creating a museum as a culminating activity was always quite fun and easily adapted to any theme. A museum of art showcased thematic projects or a museum of science exhibited experiments, offering students a chance to explain to others what they were looking at or experimenting with. A balance museum for math offered weight balance, body-balance pictures, and an interactive demonstration such as balancing a book on one hand and then both hands. We created surveys of healthy breakfasts, lunches, and dinners for investigating nutrition in health.

One year we created an ABC Book for protecting our environment. We then made a paper quilt of science concepts, "ABC OF LOVING OUR WORLD," and entered into the Environmental Protection Agency's Paul G.

Earth artists

Grady Studdard (left), Maribeth Simmons and teacher Mary Jane Devlin are proud of the winning poster their K-1 Joel School class entered in the U.S. Environmental Agency Paul G. Keough Earth Artist Program. The children used the alphabet as inspiration of ways to save the earth, and won at the state level.

Everyone feels proud to win an environmental award and see a newspaper photo of us.

Keough Earth Artist Program's competition. We won in the multi-age K-1 category in Connecticut. The children and I were filled with pride.

The Learning Web also served as a framework for the Learning Contract and students' reflections and progress evaluation of their learning, all of which is detailed later in this section. Other Integrated Day Program teachers used these Learning Webs in our work to reflect, revise, and improve our program and practices.

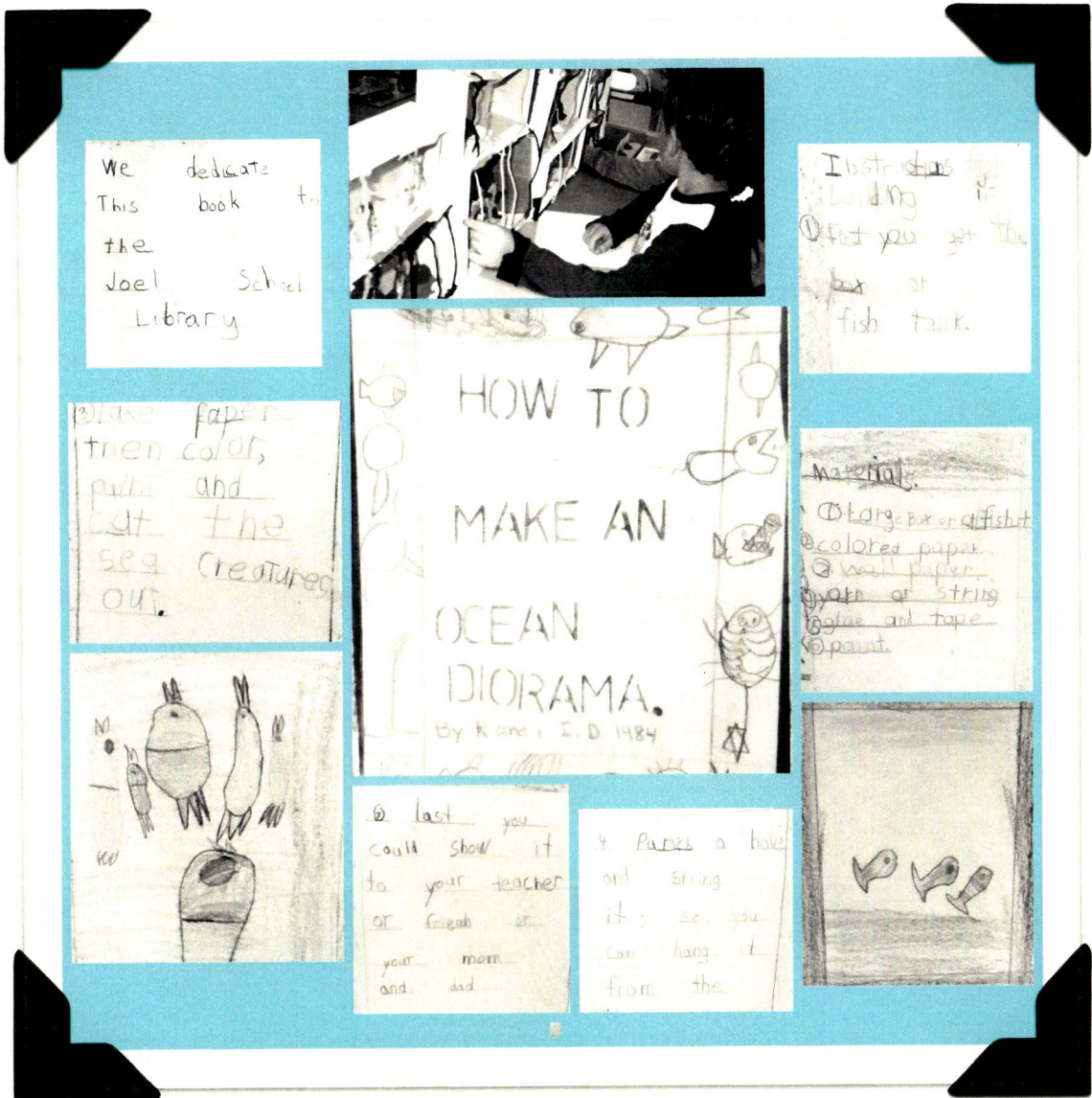

Students write a book about how to make a diorama.

Bringing the Outside World into the Classroom

The community can be a great resource for a special trip. For one thematic study, Early Americans, our class doubled with an Integrated Day Grade 4 and 5 classroom and prepared a tour of the Stanton House in Clinton, Connecticut. I collected information about the museum and told the children many stories of long ago. We learned rhymes children may have

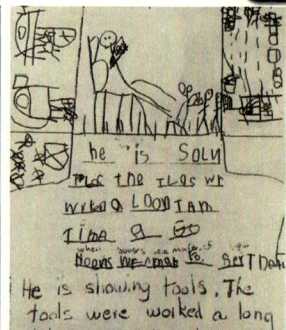

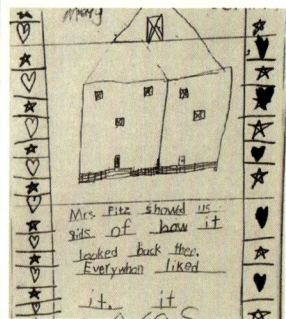

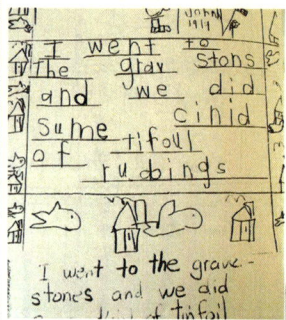

*Students sketch at the Stanton House to later write and reflect on
their favorite parts of the day.*

recited, songs they sang, and what they did for fun during eighteenth and
nineteenth century life.

Our tour of the historical museum home was an interactive, integrated
learning experience. The students dressed up and pretended to be children

from the early 1800s. We lived history through play. Children took notes and drew pictures. One of the children said, "Mrs. Devlin, there's a Humpty Dumpty in this old book." The book had an unfamiliar version:

Humpty Dumpty sat on a wall.
Humpty Dumpty had a great fall.
Four score men and four score more
Couldn't put Humpty as he was before.

The children learned to recite "Humpty Dumpty" as children in the nineteenth century learned to recite it.

On that field trip, we not only had the experience of working with students from upper grades in the Integrated Day Program and seeing the quality of their work, but we also had stories from history unfold in ways the children and I would remember. It all transpired through imaginative pretend.

After our field trip, the children planned a night tour for their parents and community. Each fourth-grade and fifth-grade student, kindergartener, and first-grade student was assigned a room in the museum. Parent volunteers dressed up as colonials to be present in each room. The museum displays valuable antiques in every room, so adults had to be vigilant. The children were fantastic and well mannered as they demonstrated respect not only for themselves but also for history.

The Learning Contract

Each student had an individual illustrated Learning Contract that addressed needed skills. The Learning Contract weaved the Learning Web with the overall curriculum. If there was an area that did not fit easily in a given Learning Contract, I saved it for a later date to use in a structured lesson or interspersed during the week as a mini-lesson.

Choice is essential to create a learning environment that supports all learners at varying stages of cognitive, social, and physical development, but as a teacher, I needed to ensure all learners were exposed to all areas of study set forth by the Board of Education. If given total charge, some students would have chosen to build with Legos all day. The Learning Contract provided accountability, ensuring each student covered all core subjects: math, science, reading, writing, and social studies. Students knew they needed to meet requirements for each area.

There are many ways to make a Learning Contract. I used a checklist format, which made it easy for students to check off completed areas. The contract allowed me to keep track of where I needed to send students during Teacher Choice time, instrumental to their learning.

The Learning Contract allowed me flexibility. I could vary curriculum areas and develop independent learning opportunities based on a student's need. If a child was ready for more challenging work, I offered an individualized math Learning Contract with more advanced work or a research opportunity providing more in-depth resources and time for discovery. On the other hand, if a child or group required extra prompting, more time for completion, or an instructional teacher intervention (re-teaching, modeling, a demonstration on how to play a game, or additional reading and writing support) I would address the specific individual's need or be part of the relevant group to help those struggling.

Because our school day was based on learning through play, I was able to personalize my teaching as needed through the Learning Contract. I also set up social conditions for learning and caring for each other. Children built trust in their self-efficacy through their ability to learn from each other. Their ownership in the class led to formation of a trusting environment. The Learning Contract allowed children to believe in the importance and purpose of their work. Students grew to become equally responsible for their learning. We shared high expectations.

After mapping out the Learning Web and negotiating a Learning Contract with each student, thematic learning took up a large part of the day. In the morning and afternoon, children had Choice Board time, when they were in charge of their learning. Most chose theme-based activities based on the Learning Web since they had come up with the ideas.

The Learning Packet

The Learning Web became part of a Learning Packet for the thematic integrated unit. In the Learning Packet was a time schedule for each day of the week including recess, lunch, physical education, art, music, library, and any other special school events. It also included a list of play themes the children developed and learning extension activities I would be sending home. For each unit, I put together bags of science experiments, language games, or audio books for home listening.

Parents responded positively to feedback forms included in each packet. They wanted to support their children and appreciated being provided with the materials and directions.

Support from home provided a foundation for our classroom to thrive. I used ideas from *Biology Experiments for Children* by Ethel Hanauer for simple science experiments such as discovering how to make carbon dioxide by blowing bubbles through a straw in a glass of water. After completing an experiment, the child could share results during share time.

One day, a child brought in her experiment and wanted to share it. I asked her to put it on my desk and told her she could share it in a little while. A few minutes later, I noticed water on the floor and wondered where it was coming from. The child said, "Oh, no! My iceberg is melting!" Needless to say, she immediately told us about her experiment.

In the Learning Packet, I also included study data or articles I came across about play. For example, I sent home ideas I learned about in *Games Children Play* by John Trivett. He states that a by-product of free play is the ability to communicate with others and form concepts, understandings, and relationships.

Children develop consciousness that learning involves interdependence, a network of relations in the mind rather than a mental collection of isolated

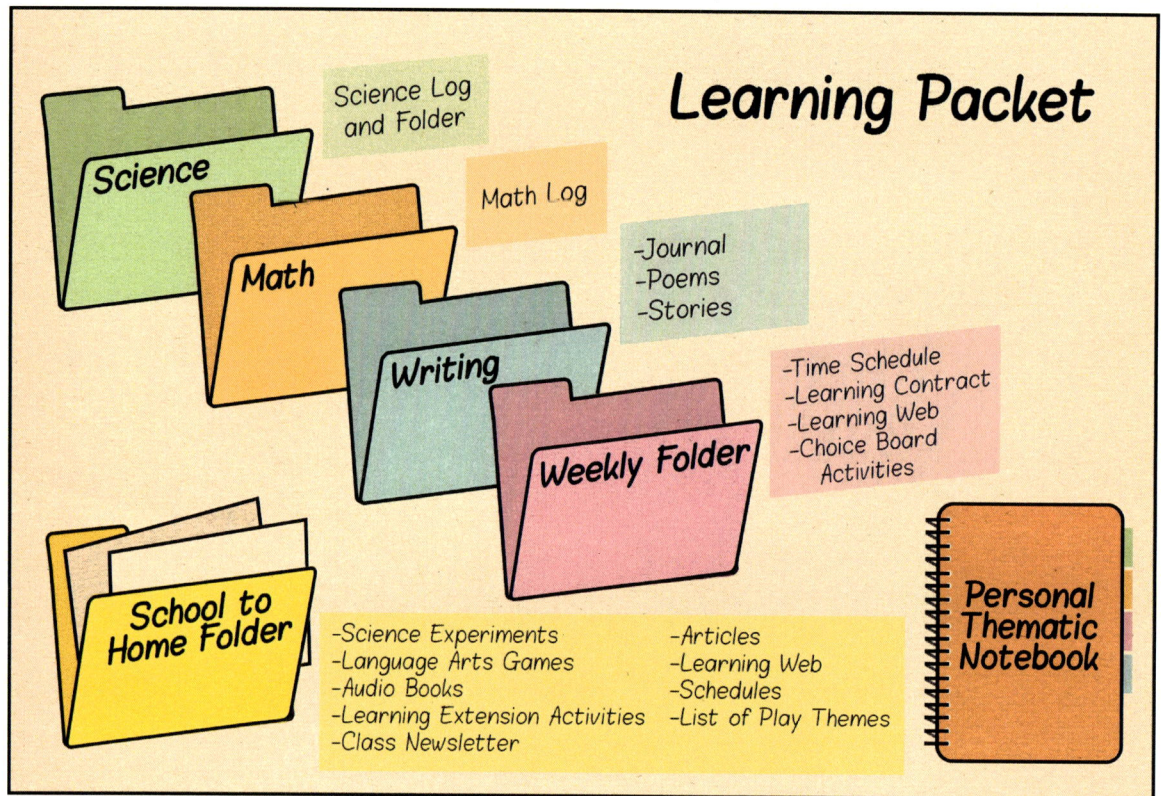

Learning packets help organize information.

facts traditionally taught in school as we try to cover the prescribed curriculum. Through integrated study, children can connect academic learning from content to needed skills and social learning. As highly engaged learners, they will store learning in their long-term memory, not just for that moment.

The Learning Packet was part of a large thematic folder that held the Learning Contract and writing notebooks, science journals, poems, and other artifacts of learning for the unit. Everything was housed in the students' color-coded drawer. This drawer or cubby held learning samples each child could use to reflect and evaluate during and at the end of the study.

Play at the Core

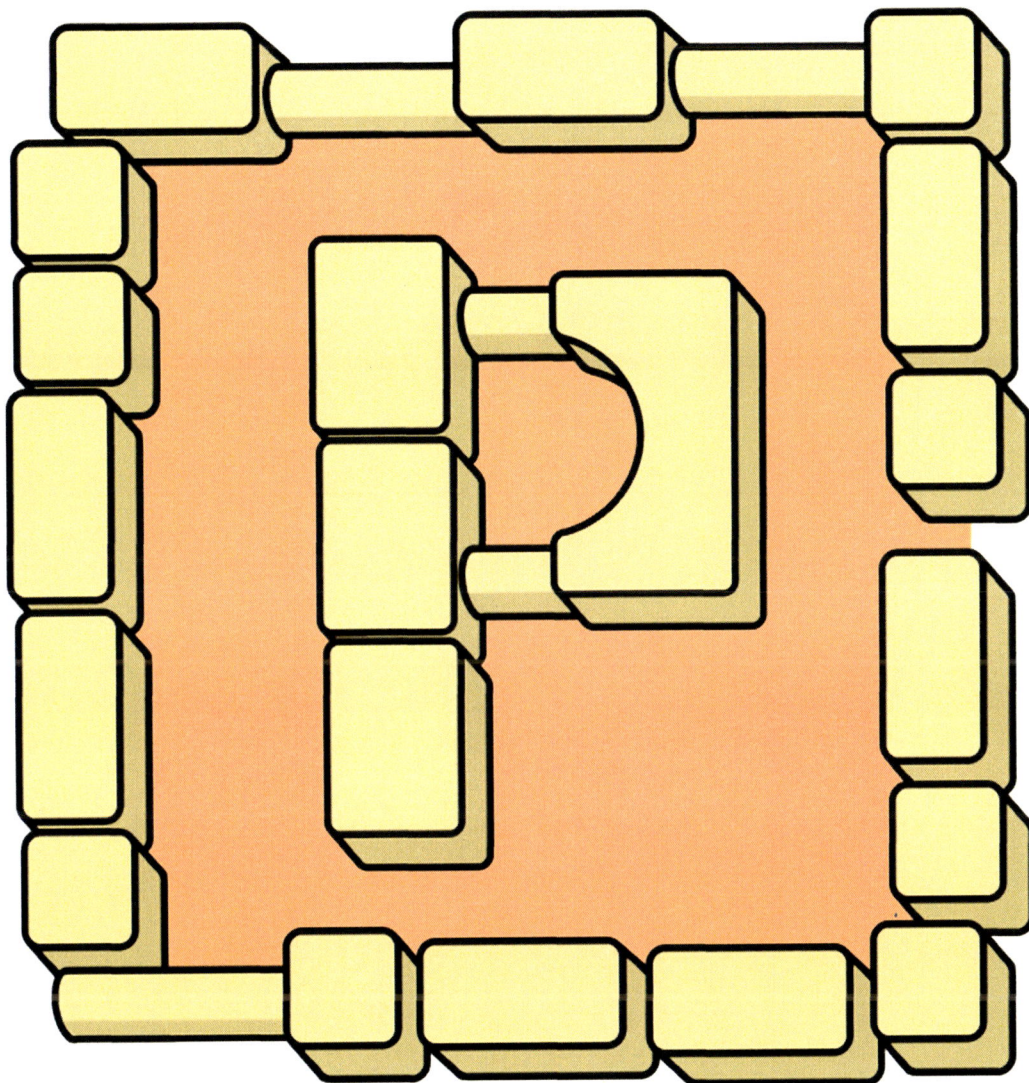

It's a happy talent to know how to play.

—Ralph Waldo Emerson

Free exploration is children's work. Each unit in our Integrated Day school year included free exploration of academic concepts to ensure ample time to look at ideas in different ways, inquire, and explore before the teacher suggested or directed another way to learn the concept. Our goal was to empower the learners and make them feel in charge of their learning, which they were. I involved children in planning each theme-based unit through the Learning Web. At the start, I knew the learning objectives, required skills, and content needed toward competency measures. I facilitated discourse to include everyone in planning, which builds in differentiation. Integrated units predicated on explorations lay the groundwork for meeting everyone's needs.

The chosen themes become powerful means of cognitive, emotional, and artistic growth. A teacher does not assist real understanding by avoiding play in order to continue traditional studies of discrete math, reading, or science activities. Even if rote responses appear correct, the ability to make solid connections and applications to other life learning is often incorrect or partial. I observed most learners did not retain rote learning for long unless there were opportunities to use the memorized information. Often, upper grade teachers complain that teachers in elementary grades don't teach what students need to know. I am convinced this is not because the material isn't taught but rather how it is taught.

Playtime in school values learning through the arts, music, and academics. The impetus toward construction of knowledge will lead to task mastery and, more importantly, unstressed children reaching their fullest potential.

Play Demonstrates Learning

Math and science teachers have long realized the importance of playing with ideas and objects. The study of math and science implores teachers to provide opportunities for children to explore materials sufficiently before suggesting that children look at them in another way. For the young child, exploring materials constitutes playing.

Playing with fraction blocks, a student learns math concepts.

One day, we didn't have enough time for Choice Board because I had planned a group math lesson. A disappointed child said, "Oh, Mrs. Devlin, we'll just do math while we are playing."

I wondered how they would pull this off, so I agreed, "Great idea." Then I passed out scrap paper for them to write down what they had learned when they were finished with math play. In the house area, children compared numbers of cups, children, and the temperature of a sick baby. Children in the block area created math equivalents using shapes and balance. The classroom gerbil had a very fast heart rate with numbers all over the place, and the group at the climber noted the concepts of "higher" and "lower."

The children were thinking like mathematicians. They came up with twenty-five different mathematical insights from their chosen areas of play. I collected what they had written down and made a booklet to show their parents, scrap paper and all. Play provides opportunities for observing, predicting, experimenting, forming hypotheses, reviewing, testing, and perhaps drawing a new conclusion.

Alphabet Play and Science

Integrating subjects makes the play environment work. Children were anxious to learn about the science equipment in our room. I came across the idea of creating a booklet called the *ABC of Science*. I decided to incorporate recognition of letters of the alphabet and sounds that make up our language while covering the science curriculum and key vocabulary.

As we established familiarity with the tools designed for meaningful scientific inquiry (such as lenses, prisms, and eye

ABCs of Science
by Mrs. Devlin's Class

A is for air.

B is for balance, bounce, and body.

C is for color, composting, and constellations.

D is for drop, dark, and discover.

E is for energy, exercise, estimate, and eggs.

F is for fat, food, and float.

G is for gravity.

H is for heavy, helicopter, and hard.

I is for ice and inch.

J is for jet and Jello.

K is for kaleidoscope and kinetic.

L is for light.

M is for magnets, metric, and measure.

N is for night and noise.

O is for oceans.

P is for planets and pendulums.

Q is for quiet.

R is for rain and rainbow.

S is for space, seasons, stars, and seeds.

T is for top.

U is for universe.

V is for volume and vibrations.

W is for weather, worms, weak, and wind.

X is for xylophone.

Y is for yo-yo.

Z is for zipper gears.

droppers), it became necessary to develop a connection between the scientific tools and their intended use. Children's understanding of their world grew. The *ABC of Science* naturally introduced language concepts and reinforced letter-sound relationships, thus providing a logical order management strategy to any scientific task. I found using the ABC method not only increased vocabulary but also increased interest.

I went through the curriculum and highlighted key terms and topics. Then I let the children figure out how to learn about them. They brainstormed, sorted, categorized, and made sense of the words—and of their world. We did not always proceed and learn in alphabetical order. We might consider *S* before *C*, for example, but in the end we put them all in alphabetical order. I also noticed many children decided to use Choice Board time studying science. Some children stapled pages together and came up with their own ABC booklets of flowers, bridges, songs, trees, rocks, or even friends.

Integrating Language Arts

Writing is a form of speaking, and reading is a form of listening to another. Reading, writing, listening, and speaking were integrated throughout each day. Children wrote and read letters, phrases, and sentences. Since children learn to hear patterns and rhymes in language more easily at five years old than at any other time in their life, I began the kindergarten year with a project on nursery rhymes and built on that foundation throughout the year. Not only was this word play, but it also supported the foundation of literacy learning, phonemic awareness. They read aloud, reported, dramatized, chanted, sang, and told about what they read or had written. Rhymes, poems, and songs enriched every theme studied.

Before daily Silent Sustained Reading, or SSR, we started with a warm-up such as singing together from song charts. Music lyrics and reading go hand in hand, so rhythm and melodies filled the room. To improve fluency, I dug far and wide for books at every reading level so everyone worked on fluency every single day. Additionally, we used partner reading, shared reading, and reading response. Readers need time to read. I witnessed them having success and falling in love with reading.

We wrote daily in our individual journals and math logs. Writing about their discoveries was part of their play. Students kept their handwritten copies of favorite poems and songs in their journals to reread often. We made versions of predictable texts, like one based on *Brown Bear, Brown Bear* by Bill Martin Jr., using our Sea Life Theme for content. We honored our writing using an author's chair where children sat while reading their writing to the class.

Writing and reading did not stay on the page or in a chair. They moved with the child. Our class generated lots of reading material, and I provided time for them to read it all aloud, showing them they completed important work.

Throughout thematic study, children wrote for their own purposes and learning. They wrote versions of songs, poems, stories, reviews, and reports. We argued, discussed, described, explored, and told stories. We spoke, drew, and wrote what we wanted to express. Children wrote constantly. We took advantage of incidental situations that arose whether social or for a cause such as when we made signs asking if anyone had seen our missing gerbil.

Whether learning pertained to letter names and sounds, words, phrases, songs, or books, I made lessons purposeful and interactive. Through board games, word play, and listening and speaking, the children engaged in learning phonics and reading. Students used their Learning Contracts to select from an array of activities. We used word lists to read and spell words related to our theme, and we played games with

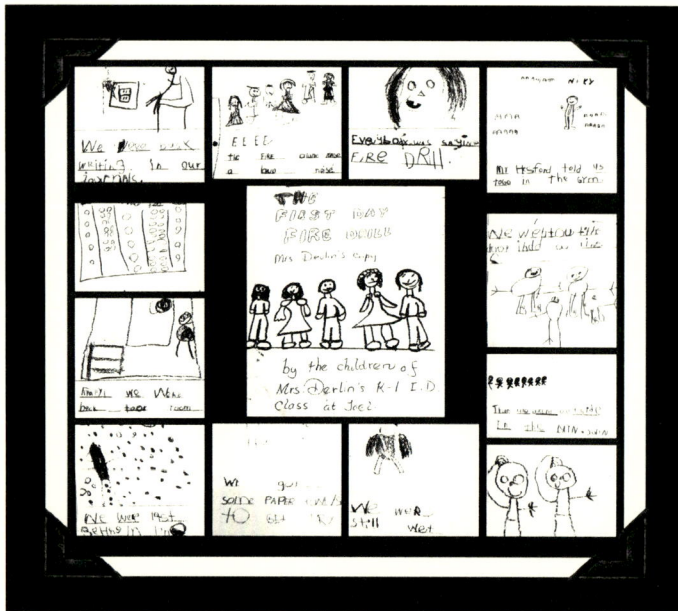

Children make a book about fire drills.

sight words that appeared hanging on walls and out in the halls. I recorded skills, strategies and competencies each student met on my master list. Occasionally, but never as a mainstay, I used worksheets if they made a connection

One student listens to another student read.

between the skill of the lesson or the thematic study. Often, I placed worksheets in a plastic sleeve for practice so children could easily correct errors if needed.

In an environment that continually asks children to put forth effort and try, they will often accept a suggestion to try new materials or ideas in their quest for knowledge. I watched for an opening and then offered suggestions, asked questions, picked out a book, or taught a skill. Such offerings help in taking away obstacles to learning so children engage in a new way of looking at solutions while reading and writing.

My observations of the students' progress were ongoing and included key elements in assessing the need for teaching reading in an integrated manner. Sometimes my observations revealed patterns. Many students, for example, ignored proper punctuation or struggled to decode certain sounds such as *aw* or *ed*. If I needed to teach a language structure, I planned lessons addressing the skill. Having a classroom of engaged, curious, critical, and imaginative thinkers who were self-sufficient learners allowed me to bring groups of children together for instruction as needed.

Play and choice-centered learning did not mean laissez-faire teaching or learning. I honored curricular requirements and developmental information to guide lessons and then tailored lessons based on the children's needs.

> *Play and choice-centered learning did not mean laissez-faire teaching or learning.*

I often received questions about whether the first graders could learn all they needed to learn about literacy while in a combined K-1 classroom. Without a doubt, each grade benefited from the other. The presence of kindergarteners in the classroom validated time for learning through play. The presence of first graders in the classroom offered opportunities for kindergarteners to learn skills and the purpose for reading and writing. Developmental and cognitive dimensions of each child had room to grow. I could nurture those who needed more time while providing challenges for those ready to fly.

A Writing Environment

In a classroom that values writing as a process, children's ideas will flourish. In a writing class that accepts less-than-perfect spelling (temporary spelling), uses storyboards, and allows oral storytelling as a prewriting expectation, the children will know their ideas are important and valued. Children should see writing not as perfecting letters and words but rather as expressing their ideas.

In a classroom that accepts rough-draft penmanship and validates the students' efforts on their first try, children will not fear they are doing it wrong. Having children see their ideas in print is the goal no matter what it takes to get there. Frustrating a child or making him or her feel badly about

Children collaborate on making a book and begin to think of themselves as writers.

writing can imprint a lasting negative effect not easily fixed. Writing is an exploration of possibilities and thoughts woven into language and words.

Acceptance of Young Writers

Children grow to want to learn to use all the tools for learning, including those of good writing. However, children don't need to be held accountable for all writing conventions at once. Just as we accepted speech attempts and responded to children when they were toddlers, so we must accept early writing attempts to encourage development of the emerging writer.

The students in Grade 1 wrote beyond my expectations. They grasped what makes a good story.

Young writers learn by trial and error. Handwriting, spelling, and writing conventions are a part of effective writing and provide opportunities to learn through self-correction. When a teacher models correct usage, provides opportunities for practice, and holds high expectations for success at the task, a child will internalize skills that will lead to mastery.

I once heard a Japanese educator comment on the American parents who constantly remind their children to say "Please" and "Thank you," basic manners. He said that in Japan, the adult never reminds young children about errors in manners. However, he said Japanese adults never allow themselves to be ill-mannered in front of their children, thereby fully expecting the children will follow modeled behavior. The same sense of expectation applies to the writing process. When children see their teacher believes they can write, they write. When children believe they have stories to tell, they write.

Oral Stories and Writing

Writing involves gathering mental collections of what learners know and experience. By telling a story out loud first, children can better transfer ideas to their journals through words and pictures. Sometimes, I used a method taught to me by our speech and language specialist, who came in to deliver a group language lesson about how to speak in full paragraphs. He brought us a poster that described how to tell a story.

The poster had a big *I* for the introduction to a story. The child had to name a subject: a person, place, or thing. The next letter on the poster was a *D* with three tails coming out from it. Each child had to say three details about what happened to the subject of the story. Next was the letter *I* again, and this time the child had to name a feeling about the story and say why he or she felt that way.

After modeling a simple event about my family and pointing to each letter on the poster, I asked the children to try. Young children always have stories to tell. They were so excited and confident following the simple model. After dividing a piece of paper by folding it into four squares, students drew an introduction in the first box, then a detail picture in the other three. I also had them put a large, crayoned-in period at the end of the picture in the fourth box. Properly placed periods increased in frequency as a result. Children drew a final reflection or feeling about the events on the back of the paper.

Drawings on folded paper employ the three-details method of storytelling.

Initially, I asked everyone to tell his or her story orally, which took a little time, but soon they could draw and write their stories more independently. They could then transfer their stories to their journals through words and pictures. The simple structure provided a road map to set them free to write.

Many five-year-old students have not yet developed the fine motor coordination to manage pencil and paper tasks easily, and even some six-year-olds are not ready. In my classroom, children who were not able write or form

Today, we went to the beach. Mrs. Devlin liked watching the children cooperate in building the most complex system of rivers, dams, and pools she had ever seen.

After a day at the beach, children make drawings to tell their stories about the day.

letters easily, dictated stories to me or a classroom volunteer. The computer solved many problems. One child, not ready to write, said, "I'll tell you what letters to write, and you can type them." The child felt like a writer, which was the goal. The confidence and imagination of those young writers grew. They felt empowered to write.

A Modeling Procedure for Cooperative Group Sharing

I liked to use Show and Tell for the first modeling procedure as a way to orally tell a story. I began with the job of being recorder. Demonstrating the recorder's job helps the children plan and rehearse what they will share.

Initial modeling can occur in a fishbowl setting. The procedure started with me, as recorder, choosing two children to share something. I designated my spot to meet by the easel. The two children came with me while the class watched. The three of us, the modeling group, sat at a small table facing each other. The other children watched and learned the procedure. I explained by thinking aloud and modeled what I did for each step.

I folded a piece of paper in four; then I wrote the first child's initials in the top corner of the rectangle. The first child told me his or her Show and Tell. I quickly recorded a simple drawing of what she or he had shared. Children can state details verbally, but the drawing must be simple. Notes are for the recorder to use to remember what was shared. The recorder is the only one with a pencil and the only one to write initials or draw.

I repeated the process for the second child. Then, talking aloud to myself, I said, "Now we can go back to the group meeting area. I'll sit in the place designated for the recorder."

I shared with the class the first student's story: "Sara shared about the treasure she got for her birthday. Chris shared about the new football his big brother gave him."

I then switched roles and modeled how to be a listener.

The goal is to have the class working in small groups with designated recorders, who will share with the larger group when the class comes together.

The process takes from five to seven minutes in all. Results lead to children working cooperatively. All children have an opportunity to talk, listen, and form main ideas. Each student has a turn taking notes as the recorder.

I typically began the cooperative group sharing procedure by modeling it through Show and Tell. I sometimes used the same process for problem solving or a Book Talk. Children could tell about an independent reading book or a thematic study book. I've also used the sharing process for gathering and assembling graphing data and the end-of-the-day evaluation.

Such a sharing technique works well for small groups to reflect upon and share what they learn working together in their play area. The procedure takes time for the children to learn, but once they become familiar with the process, they show an increase in focus and attention to details. They remember ideas and meaningfully sequence them. Children increase their ability to relay organized ideas to an audience. They develop language, reading, and writing skills that will benefit them all through their learning.

Show and Tell and Storytelling

I provided time for Show and Tell every day, an integral part of the program. That way if students brought in a story or something related to the theme, they were able to share it with the class. Stories or short statements can be expanded using "Pass the Wand." A student passes the wand. Then the next student develops and adds on to the original story. A variation I tried was to put theme objects in the center of the circle. A child picked up an object and started the story. Then each child drew or wrote a next part on scrap paper to be ready when it was time for that part. The stories were engaging!

The object being passed can be a fanciful or a thematic object that lends itself to magic, such as a Native American feather that tells the story of where it has been. The teacher or a child can give the setting for the story. The children add characters and plot as the story unfolds.

When introducing the concept of creating a story, the teacher must provide leads or ongoing questions such as how, what, where, when, and why.

As the children become more proficient, they can build a series of events and not solve the conflict or problem until they are almost through the complete circle. The story can be enjoyed by itself on its own terms, written down, or recorded, so large or small groups can listen and discuss it.

Some of my observations about storytelling include:

- Language defines us as human beings. We use language to process all thoughts of which we are capable. We each digest our own life experience in narrative, whether or not we have a listener. This brings us closer to meaning, our touchstone to reality, and constitutes our being. Storytelling establishes an essential relationship between teller and listener.

- Children *must* have stories told to them. Stories are *vital* to their health, well-being, and development. Stories are entertaining yet never an extra or a frill. Storytelling may not be identified as a specific line item in the curriculum but is at the heart of learning.

- Children need to become storytellers themselves. The more they understand the structure of story and hear the richness of language, the more meaning they will bring to their own lives.

- Children become storytellers if they listen to stories, but they need models. A teacher does not have to know many stories, and they need not be long. A story can (and should) be retold many times to the point when the students can retell the story with details.

- Reading stories aloud is excellent but is not the same as storytelling. A spoken story is processed by the storyteller, not learned word for word. The story has something of the teller in it. The story is also very special. It is something the teller has taken the trouble to reach into his or her memory for, to share with the listeners. The story has importance. Children love to *listen* to stories. They engage in the process, and they are learning.

Valuing Listening

Listening shares equal status with reading, writing, speaking, and viewing in language arts. Children will find success listening and responding either in writing or orally when there is a purpose for listening. If the children's response takes the form of oral questions and answers, a long enough wait time leads to greater success and more thoughtful responses.

Rarely do young children sit and listen for long without responding, moving, or interacting in some way. It's natural at their age. The teacher is responsible to make sure the group accepts the expectation of sitting quietly while making sure it does not become a burden to the children. Just as we want children to be thoughtful, the teacher must also be thoughtful that young people need to move after a time. Keeping the learning moving while offering active involvement is the secret to getting students to listen.

Fostering Listening Skills

reading shared poetry or nursery rhymes

stories read or told by another

singing entire song or chant

repeating back a single line

audio books on the computer

teacher-recorded books or made-up stories

recordings of their own voice

recorded music heard while reading song lyrics

cooperative learning groups

responding to group shares on any topic

Show-and-Tell time

telling stories

purposefully viewing videos or visuals

finding details while viewing videos or viewing visuals

peer talking with expected feedback

politely serving as audience for performances

responding to another's delivery

Simple Listening Games

Echo Game

calling on a child randomly to

repeat what another child said

Paraphrase Game

similar to the Echo Game,

but the child puts the heard statement into

his or her own words

Activities that foster good listening require children to look at the speaker and, while not talking, attend to what the speaker is saying. "Look and listen, but don't talk when someone else is speaking" is a great motto for a class. They will soon know and repeat expectations for good listening. The best listening occurs when the teacher and children agree on how to listen and when core values of trust, caring, and responsibility for responding are shared and expected.

Observation Games
Observe by Sight

Children pass an object around a circle and, one at a time, say one attribute of the item.
No one may repeat exactly what has already been said, although
a child may say a different word that describes the same attribute, for example,
"round" and "a circle" may both be used.
The Observe Game can be used with other senses.

Observe by Touch

A child reaches into a hidden area and observes only by feel.
Cut the toe off a large sock and stretch the remaining sock over
a coffee can or use a box to hide objects.

Observe by Sound

Children determine what's hidden in a container by sound.
Pass the covered container with something in it and
each child gives a similar description.

Observe by Smell

Children determine by smell what's hidden in a container.
Children may want to try this version after they play the others. Put something with a strong smell in a small plastic container with a few holes in the lid. Comments will be humorous.

Observe by Taste

Children determine what an unknown substance is by taste.
This game is best done in small groups with individual portions of things to taste.
Participants comment to each other.

Managing a Choice Classroom

Many teachers have asked me how I managed such an active learning environment. A program with high child input into the design and implementation of a curriculum requires systematic classroom management with consistent behavioral expectations. I saw each student coming into the classroom with his or her own way of thinking, and I outlined clear and fair consequences for unwise choices.

The simple task of giving children responsibility for their own actions led to a consistent way of disciplining in our classroom. Being respectful and firm with the rules owned by all learners, including me, was most effective. The system of listing consequences had the benefit of keeping discipline in the fact arena and, with all parties involved, removing emotional overtones.

By keeping to the facts, I communicated to children in our classroom the expectations the Board of Education had of me as a teacher in our school. I was responsible for the curriculum, materials, and time needed to teach. I asked the children, "What is your job?" They brainstormed their expectations for behavior that would allow everyone to learn as much as possible and, more importantly, provide time for choices in learning.

Together, we developed a list. First, I listed positive, expected behaviors they thought of, and then I listed consequences they came up with and added my own for disruptive or thoughtless behavior. I posted the list to refer to when necessary. I sent a copy home to parents so they would be aware of the learning strategy.

Since I provided a large block of time for each child to choose from a selected array of learning options, a natural consequence of not following expected behavior was to lose Choice Board time. I observed a child closely when he or she did not follow expected behavior, and if there was an attempt at appropriate behavior, I provided an immediate, random reward. So a child who repeatedly lost some of his or her Choice Board time was able to earn some of it back by displaying desirable behavior.

Not every infraction needs a consequence. Sometimes, it is enough simply to call a child over, whisper a friendly reminder to take notice of inappropriate behavior, and ask if he or she can control the behavior. Calling a student over with a reminder about a behavior not on the list can work magic and, thus, the list works well.

I did not list on the classroom chart how I would handle individual cases when they involved losing more than one Choice Board time. Most often, losing one Choice Board took care of inappropriate behavior.

The children were in charge of their behavior, and their positive behavior reaped a positive reaction from me. I used a method of discipline that allowed more time for teaching and less time for discipline. Over time, students demonstrated increased responsibility for self-discipline. Of course, sometimes a behavior would still be off the charts when emotion factored in. I taught them strategies for coping during such times: leaving a situation, naming a problem, or discussing possible solutions that would enable children to become more capable teenagers and adults able to handle situations with respect for self and others.

> *They looked.*
> *They listened.*
> *They questioned.*
> *Then . . .*
> *They made.*
> *They became.*
> *They understood.*
> *They learned.*
> *Then . . .*
> *They shared their knowledge.*

Mrs. Devlin's Core Belief:
"I am in charge of myself"

CONSEQUENCES FOR BEHAVIOR

Consequences for Appropriate Behavior

• being responsible for yourself, of being your own boss •

• learning as much as possible •

• setting a good example •

• feeling happy and making others happy •

• earning five extra minutes of Choice Board time •

(at teacher discretion)

Consequences for Inappropriate Behavior

• removal from the group to think and return when ready •

• loss of some Choice Board time •

• loss of whole Choice Board time •

• loss of recess •

• choice card to the principal with a note from teacher •

• call or letter home and possible meeting with parents and you •

Choosing to Care and Trust

The only real mistake is one from which we learn nothing.

—Henry Ford

To build trust, we need love. We expect that children will learn from problems that arise when they play. A misguided choice does not need to threaten self-esteem in the atmosphere of play: children overlook the choice, incorporate it, or change the context of it. Students trust their teacher to understand and respond with empathy to decisions they make.

In life, people make mistakes and correct them. Children use mistakes and their own logic to refine their responses. Learning from mistakes offers a way for people to learn. Toddlers learn to walk and talk by approximating what they perceive. Moms and dads praise successful attempts to walk and encourage toddlers to try again when they fall. Everyone expects mistakes and accepts them as part of the learning process.

Learning is recursive, based on repeated attempts that grow ever more successful. Trusting that it is okay to make mistakes and trusting in eventual success strengthens one's ability to try, and try again.

Teachers establish teaching goals by observing each student's learning and behavior needs. A teacher must model expected behaviors in the classroom. Mistakes will happen. Children make mistakes. How teachers view and respond to a mistake will influence how students learn and respond to a mistake, the key to creating trust.

Repairing Trust through Reflection and Dramatic Play

A child can unintentionally hurt another child's feelings during a play activity. Sometimes, during a post evaluation meeting after Choice Time, a child brought up a problem. To address a social issue or "hurt," we convened an evaluation meeting, a class meeting, or a small group meeting to address unintentional physical encounters and intentional, unkind interactions. Physical hurt, even when a true accident, still hurts and must be addressed.

An intentional misdeed breaks trust. Once the teacher recognizes broken trust, the teacher must state to the students involved that trust has been temporarily broken. The teacher must then mediate the misdeed and state how trust can be earned again. Students realize the hurt is real and learn not to hold hurt inside but instead deal with it. At an evaluation meeting, a time to talk about issues, any party to what happened can suggest appropriate solutions, and the child with hurt feelings can suggest a resolution. After discussion, often with aggrieved parties only, I picked the most helpful solution and the child who caused the hurt chose or accepted a consequence.

Often offering "I'm sorry for . . . " is all that is needed when the words have a sincere meaning. No child wants anyone mad at him or her. All must value trust. Although the choice of continuing to play in the activity goes away for the day, the next day is a new day with a fresh start, which means all is forgiven.

Learning about trust can be integrated into a play activity. For example, from one behavior evaluation meeting, I wrote a plot for a future puppet show. I often wrote puppet shows to explain a problem. "Breaking Trust" was a puppet show I wrote about an imaginary incident where trust was given and broken between two children in a play situation. I did the first puppet show alone, but if other incidents occurred in class, the children themselves named the problem and talked about it through puppets.

In the puppet show on the next page, two children processed a personal response. Alex and Sam realized if they hurt each other's feelings, they wouldn't be able to play and have fun. They realized they could compromise and make it work so they would both be happy.

At the end of any puppet show, children provided comments about the story, the actors speaking, the presentation, and the scenery. They offered suggestions about making it a better show. Children gave me appropriate congratulations for my performance of "Breaking Trust." They could relate to Sam and Alex because they had been in similar situations. Others in the class learn from viewing, processing, and responding to the puppet show.

Saying "I'm sorry" is too easily and thoughtlessly said much too often. I wanted to have children become more aware of their ability to control their own responses with kindness and trust. My goal was to have trust present in all their interactions so they would grow to solve problems during emotionally challenging situations. I observed children asking for the gift of

A Puppet Show
Breaking Trust

Characters: Narrator, Alex, Sam

Narrator: *Two children are playing in the house area. Alex and Sam had been playing and preparing dinner. Alex and Sam both wanted to cook. Instead of naming the problem and looking for a solution, Sam got angry, and Alex felt* sad.

Sam: I'm going to cook because you can't cook soup at all. It always tastes terrible. I won't eat it.

Narrator: *Alex's feelings were hurt. What a big problem, not only hurting someone's feelings but breaking the trust that problems will be solved kindly.*

Alex: I want to cook. I am a good cook. I help my mommy at home.

Sam: No, I am cooking. You can't cook.

Narrator: *Alex starts to cry and throws down the spoon.*

Alex: You hurt my feelings. I'm not playing.

Narrator: *Sam doesn't want the game to end. They've had fun up until now.*

Sam: I'm sorry.

Alex: Anyone can say they're sorry. How do I know you really mean it?

Sam: I was unkind, and I want to be kind. I want you to give me a gift of trust that I will be kind again.

Alex: Okay, I will trust you to be kind. We can take turns cooking.

Sam: I bet I'll like what you're going to make.

Alex: I bet you will, too, because it's your favorite meal. I'm making pizza!

> *My goal was to have trust present in all their interactions so they would grow to solve problems during emotionally challenging situations.*

trust many times. Asking for the gift of trust is a different way of asking for forgiveness. As a teacher, I didn't need to get involved in their quarrels or make any new rules.

When children capitalize on their capacity for compassion added with their imagination, they can build trust in the most important people of all, themselves.

Children learn to believe in trust. They learn they can resolve conflicts in a manner that builds confidence and autonomy in the learner and trust among peers. I have learned important lessons from my students.

Lessons Learned about Caring and Building Trust

On my first day teaching, a child repeating kindergarten did not want to have any part of the school scene. I felt nervous and excited as the other twenty-nine people entered the classroom. I had difficulty welcoming the children because that one little student refused to cooperate, running around the room, screaming, "You hate my guts."

I watched as the other children became unsure and nervous.

So, I said, "No, I love your guts. I just don't love the behavior you're choosing."

The student marveled and questioned repeatedly, "You love my guts?" and made a decision to give the new situation a chance, for which I was grateful. I not only loved this student's guts, but I also gave the student the choice to have the uncooperative behavior loved. We began to build a foundation of trust. I had to honor and nurture that trust.

When adults in a child's life see what might be viewed as misbehavior as an opportunity to learn and care, adults promote trust. When a child's peers participate in exploring and solving each other's problems, a caring and trusting community gains strength. Whether small or serious, problems always provide opportunities to learn.

One kindergartner, usually well-behaved, was discovered taking children's snacks out of their backpacks. Many children were jealous of the sweet treats some children brought to school for snack. My mouth watered at times for a favorite treat, and I was well beyond the egocentric stage.

I told the child it was wrong to take a classmate's property, and I placed all snacks on a high shelf to solve the problem. Class discussions about not taking what belongs to another and consequences did not change the child's behavior. What started out as a poor choice blossomed into troublesome behavior.

I decided to teach the students about Transactional Analysis (TA) by Eric Berne, MD, who defines any social interaction as a transaction. In *Description of Transactional Analysis*, Berne writes:

> If two or more people encounter each other, . . . sooner or later one of them will speak or give some other indication of acknowledging the presence of the others. This is called transactional stimulus. Another person will then say or do something which is in some way related to the stimulus, and that is called the transactional response.

Berne says each person has three ego states: parent, adult, and child. I explained to the class how TA helps people solve problems they are facing by understanding themselves better. I explained to the class:

> We all have three ways of behaving that are good and needed at times: the parent behavior, the child behavior, and the adult behavior. Some behaviors are good, but other behaviors can hurt a friend. We can behave like parents who observe the situation and tell us what we should do to keep us healthy and safe. Teachers often use the parent self because it is their job to warn you if something is unsafe, as when they say, "Keep the scissors pointed down when you are carrying them."
> Then there is the child behavior. We all have a child behavior, even grownups. Child behavior is special because we feel, act, and learn there. We feel happy, loving, sad, or excited, which are all part of being human. We can also feel angry or jealous and do things that please us in the child behavior stage, even if those things are not good for us and hurtful to others. For example, "I like cookies. My friend has cookies. I want them."

The third behavior that can help us all be kind and thoughtful without emotion is called the adult behavior. The adult behavior processes the child and adult reactions to make an informed decision. It is the place where we talk and listen to facts. The adult figures out how to solve the problem. Even children can choose to act like an adult.

I then drew a stick figure each of a parent, a child with a big heart, and an adult with big ears. We stated the problem in our adult part: children's snacks are being taken. If we listened as a child, that didn't work because a child can only feel and would probably feel jealous and want the snacks. If we listened as a parent, we'd tell ourselves that taking someone else's snacks is wrong. The adult part has to listen to both the child and parent to solve the problem.

As a class, we solved the problem while having fun with dramatic play, acting out being the parent, the child, and the adult. Later, I approached the child taking the snacks about the snack problem. The adult stated the problem: the children's snacks are being taken. A child would go to get his or her snack, but there would be no snack to eat because someone else had taken it. How can we solve the problem? The snack taker listened enthralled and thought as an adult and the snacks were never taken again. I did not need to send the child to the principal or make the child feel like a bad person to solve the problem.

Transactional Analysis is much more complex than explained in this context; I adapted the concept for classroom use. I tried to get students to think about how they reacted to situations and for the snack taker to reflect on the inappropriate, hurtful actions. Transactional Analysis worked as a powerful tool for expanding awareness of thinking about mistakes and increasing options to develop appropriate behaviors. The process was in line with the practice of learning through play the children experienced together in their integrated study. Like a child's work of play, Transactional Analysis involved acting while interacting and reacting to the learning with imagination and cognition fully engaged.

I wrote a letter to all parents explaining that sending in snacks had created problems because some children envied special snacks and often it took too much time to consume them. Instead I requested donations of healthy snacks or money from each parent once a month, and I purchased graham crackers, saltines, apples, carrots, and other healthy snacks. Unless there was a dietary requirement, I did not allow snacks brought from home, which created a more harmonious atmosphere during snack time.

Trusting and Caring with Clear Expectations

Children's acceptance of trust provides a non-threatening teaching opportunity. Trust builds around the threefold understanding that:

- everyone will follow rules for expected behaviors in school
- everyone is kind to each other
- everyone will be safe and be able to learn

In the defined environment, children are not only free to talk about their feelings but are also expected to explain how something said or done by another person hurts their feelings. If students learn early their feelings are important and listened to, they will understand each other and will empathize with other perspectives when they are older and trying to understand their children, spouses, employers, or employees. Children learn to expect trust from all members of the class and to trust themselves. Such work sets the foundation for problem-solving as children grow and mature.

Teachers are instrumental in creating communities of learners who share the responsibility of building a trusting environment where children can play with kindness and safety. When a teacher genuinely likes children, shows respect for their dignity, and trusts their ability to learn, the teacher can share in their enjoyment of learning.

A teacher prepares students to be caring, conscientious, and contributing citizens by spending each moment in school as a caring, conscientious, and contributing citizen in the family-like community created in the classroom. The children and I created a child-centered, welcoming class.

Invitation to Play and Learn

A boy new to my class needed a great deal of direction. He was unsure about what would happen if he made a mistake. When it came time for him to choose an area to play

> *When a teacher genuinely likes children, shows respect for their dignity, and trusts their ability to learn, the teacher can share in their enjoyment of learning.*

from our Choice Board, he needed help. As I questioned where he would like to go and play, he said he liked the house area. I helped him put his name on the house hook on the Choice Board and took him over to the area. He held back saying, "I don't know how to play."

"Let's see what the other children are doing," I said.

One child greeted him with, "Hi. What do you want to be?"

He repeated he did not know how to play. The other child did not lecture him, just told him they needed a dog. He said he did not know how to be a dog.

A student said, "You just get under the table, and if you want something, you bark." He got under the table. I watched for a minute, then left to supervise elsewhere. When I looked again, he was an uncle coming home from work for supper. Evidently, he had solved his problem because the children trusted he would have the ability to add to the game, and eventually, he himself trusted his ability.

Building trust is a complex addition to the definition of play. It involves a child trusting himself or herself, trusting the teacher, trusting the environment and trusting— with an ability to respond to unexpected situations—social melding with other children. The desire in all humans for love and attention in the strong, ego-centered young child makes it a challenge to build trust.

Building trust means learning not to accept failure. Henry Ford once said, "Failure is the opportunity to begin again, more intelligently . . . . "

Through play, children rehearse and develop competencies and solve problems in relationships with other people and their environment. Language becomes more proficient as children communicate feelings and thoughts during play situations. They more readily consider and accept cultural ideas that differ from their own when they experience other perspectives through play. They reach meaningful understanding as they construct knowledge and a deeper acquaintance with self.

In a play atmosphere of trust, there are no bad ideas. Even if a child's idea may not be the group's choice, someone may remember it another time or in another place. Children learn very young they may choose to agree or disagree with another person's ideas but they have a right to have their own ideas.

In my class, the children witnessed my enthusiasm about the many different ideas they generated. Ideas are too precious not to be considered. I shared with the students that prestigious corporations have brain trusts. I told the children that employers paid such experts to generate lucrative and unusual ideas in their jobs. The experts simply had to share their ideas.

Sea Life
A Sample Thematic Unit

The ability to create and express is as important to the mind as physical exercise is to the body.

—Geraldine Brain Siks

A Sea Life Theme was a favorite unit of study for the students and me. We transformed our room into a seascape of learning. To begin, as with any unit, we had to get organized. I used color-coded folders—nothing fancy, just large sheets of oaktag folded in half. The folders resembled a file cabinet filled with products and artifacts of learning. A unit folder held all the colored content area folders. Some folders went back and forth between school and home. If I wanted the children to get their writing folder, it was easy to say, "Please, go get your blue folder," because all their writing folders were blue. I used colors to make organizing easy.

I set up an area for students to collect and save all of their artifacts, packets, folders, and notebooks. In my classroom, each student had a color-coded drawer to house their materials and work.

The Sea Life Theme Learning Web

For this Learning Web, the children and I discussed Choice Board activities for creative arts, language arts, math, science, social studies, physical education, music, and field trips. The children decided they wanted to paint seascapes. We honed questions: What color is at the bottom of the ocean? What would be in a seascape? What fish live in the sea? What do fish eat? What other sea life lives in the ocean?

During this inquiry about the sea, we also needed to figure out necessary materials such as colors of paint to make a sea mural. We posed research questions we would return to throughout the unit. As the teacher, I built on students' input and questions while linking outcomes to curriculum objectives.

Having a purpose for learning is important. What would we do with our learning? While working on the Learning Web, we talked about what we might do as a culminating activity. Students came up with the idea of a Waterworks Gala Performance. Knowing they would be presenting their learning motivated them to do their best work. We planned to share what we learned with our school community and families. We revisited our Learning

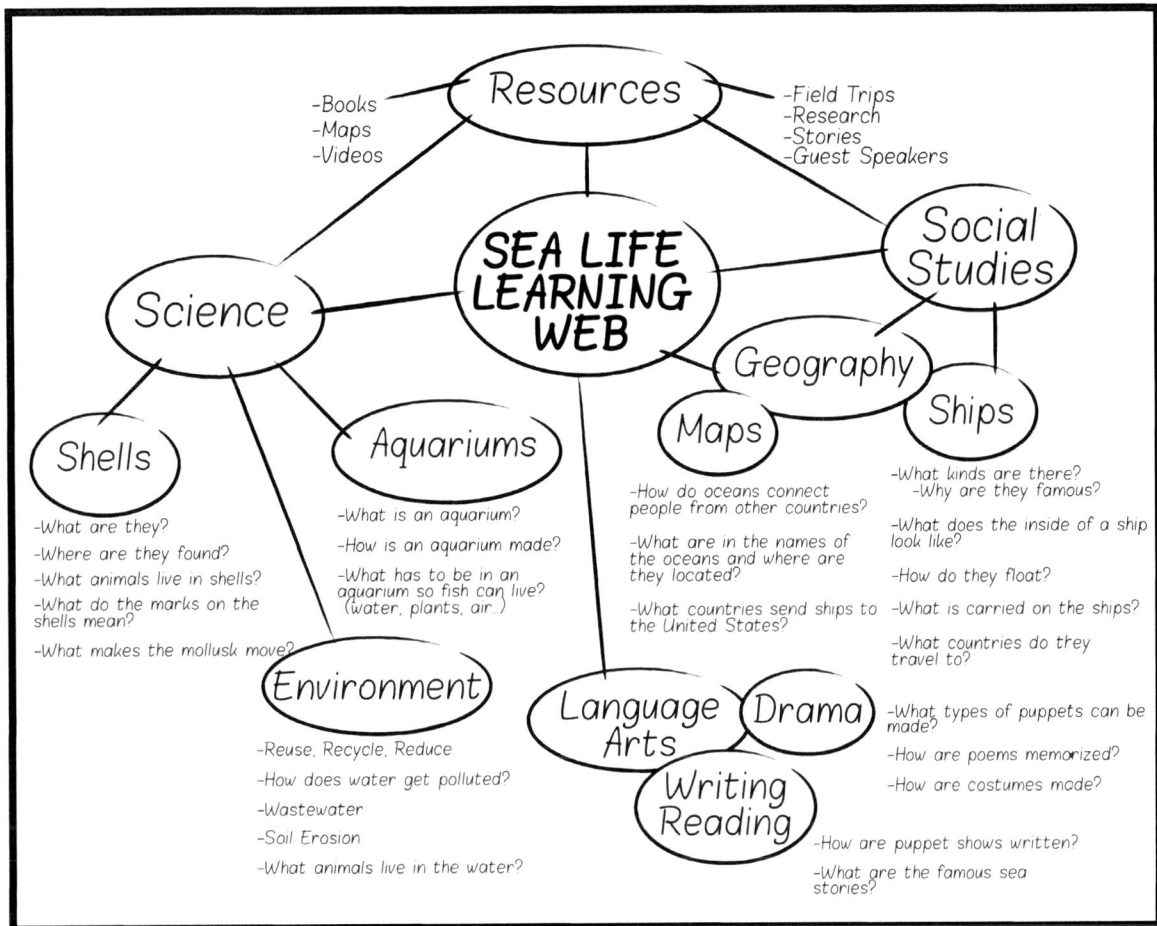

The learnng web helps with planning activities.

Web throughout the unit to plan what we would include in our Gala event. Since we worked on our end products throughout the unit, the children were filled with excitement and anxious to get started.

Sea Life Theme Learning in the Real World

During the Learning Web planning, we also discussed any field trips that we might learn from. While on a field trip to Clinton Town Beach, we studied sea animals, water, and, of course, sand. Some students collected shells. One group built sand structures while another group began digging a waterway that soon attracted many more children to join in the digging. They dug down to black muck and poured seawater into the dug out channels.

Children ran to the water and retrieved pails and pails of water to keep water in the channels moving down to the sea. They used sand and water wheels. Children's muddy clothing gave proof of involvement while they followed the "wet ankles only" rule.

The field trip provided the class with a shared experience that incorporated reading, writing, math, science, cooperative group work, and character building. Making a waterway offered a real life experience I could draw upon during future learning about ground water or erosion.

When we returned to school, the chaperones stayed at school with us and sometimes added information. We wrote stories about our day. As each student dictated a story about the beach, I typed them up. The children then took a copy of their accounts of the day home with a picture they drew. Since I hoped the children would share more about their day with their parents, I added a paragraph about the learning experience and asked parents to read the story with their children.

Children and I agree, for safety, they would go into the ocean only up to their ankles.

Sea Life Learning Materials

The Learning Packet

Learning Web and Choice Board Activities

The unit folder held color-coded content folders and logs.

Math Folder Labeled Sea Math

The folder held children's collections of math projects and a math log to record their understanding of math concepts.

The Sea Math Folder went home weekly.

Science Folder and Science Log

The folder held science logs filled with children's notations of each experiment, including predictions and actual outcomes of their in-school science experiments.

Writing Journal

The journal was a source of ongoing writing activity used for story ideas or self-authored poems and collections of rough drafts of materials that may or may not have been published.

Sea Life Spiral-Bound Notebook

The spiral-bound notebook held personal-interest sea-life material that became a book at the end of the study unit. Students collected factual information about the sea or sea topic and pictures with a sentence or two explaining each picture. They published sea poems and chanteys. The notebook included an official dedication and about-the-author page.

In addition to a field trip to our town beach, we enjoyed field trips to Mystic Aquarium and Hammonassett State Park.

We had other opportunities to learn and present our sea knowledge outside of the classroom. We accepted an invitation to Wesleyan University's Gifted Children's Festival, where we were listed on the program as "The Noontime Entertainment." It was quite an experience for the children.

We presented ourselves using adapted improvisational drama, an idea from the late Barbara Goodwille, a creative dramatist from Connecticut State University. The concept of improvisational drama involves someone calling on someone else with a question, whereby—in the classroom—the designated student responds with a movement. Then the student calls on another who responds, and so on. Each child can freely choose a question as long as it stays on theme. There are so many variations to this game, but all must follow the same procedure using the same theme or idea. For example, we used a short chant in our Sea Life Theme. I said, in set rhythm, "Emily, how do you want us to say your name?" Emily responded with her name and a motion, such as twirling around or bending up and down like a wave, and all the children repeated her name and motion. Then, Emily asked another student the same question, and that child chose a motion, perhaps crawling like a crab or shooting water out of a whale's spout. The audience enjoyed our presentation. I was so proud of them.

The students were familiar with the game because we often used a version of it for taking attendance in the classroom. I sometimes used a variation of it for a content review. The student stated his or her name, and then I asked, "What ocean do you want to say?" or "What kind of ship do you want us to sail?" or "What kind of fish do you want us to be?" The student answered, and then I asked another student a question. If someone got stuck, I helped. The game was a great transition activity.

After the Learning Web was complete and activities brainstormed with the children, I then created the Choice Board activities. I placed cards for each activity with directions or suggestions at the play area.

Sea Life Choice Board

Water Works Gala Presentation (center top)

- "The Lobster Quadrille" by Lewis Carroll performance
- Peter Pan Performance
- Write a book about how to make an aquarium

SEA LIFE CHOICE BOARD
ACTIVITIES & CULMINATING PROJECTS

Math
- Tangrams and Geoboards
- How many cubes long are different fish?
- Patterns shells ABAB or AABB, etc.
- Order by number
- Sort by color, size, type, texture

Language Arts

READING
- Research about a famous ship
- Ocean life
- Read sea stories and poems

WRITING
- Logs
- Journals
- Sea Stories
- Poetry: Haiku and Cinquain
- Sea Puppet Stories

DRAMA
- "The Lobster Quadrille"
- Peter Pan

Art

DESIGN & CREATE
- an aquarium
- clay fish
- a milk carton boat
- paint a sea mural
- seashell mobile

Climber

Design Sea Life
- sewn paper fish
- jellyfish, coral, starfish, mermaid
- treasure chest
- air tank

Science

WATER EXPERIMENTS
- hot/cold
- sink/float
- salt water/regular water/drinking water
Observe a fish: scales, gills, eyes and print it with real ink

Social Studies
- Play map game: locate and name oceans and countries
- Match products and ships with countries
- Keep a captain or crew travel log

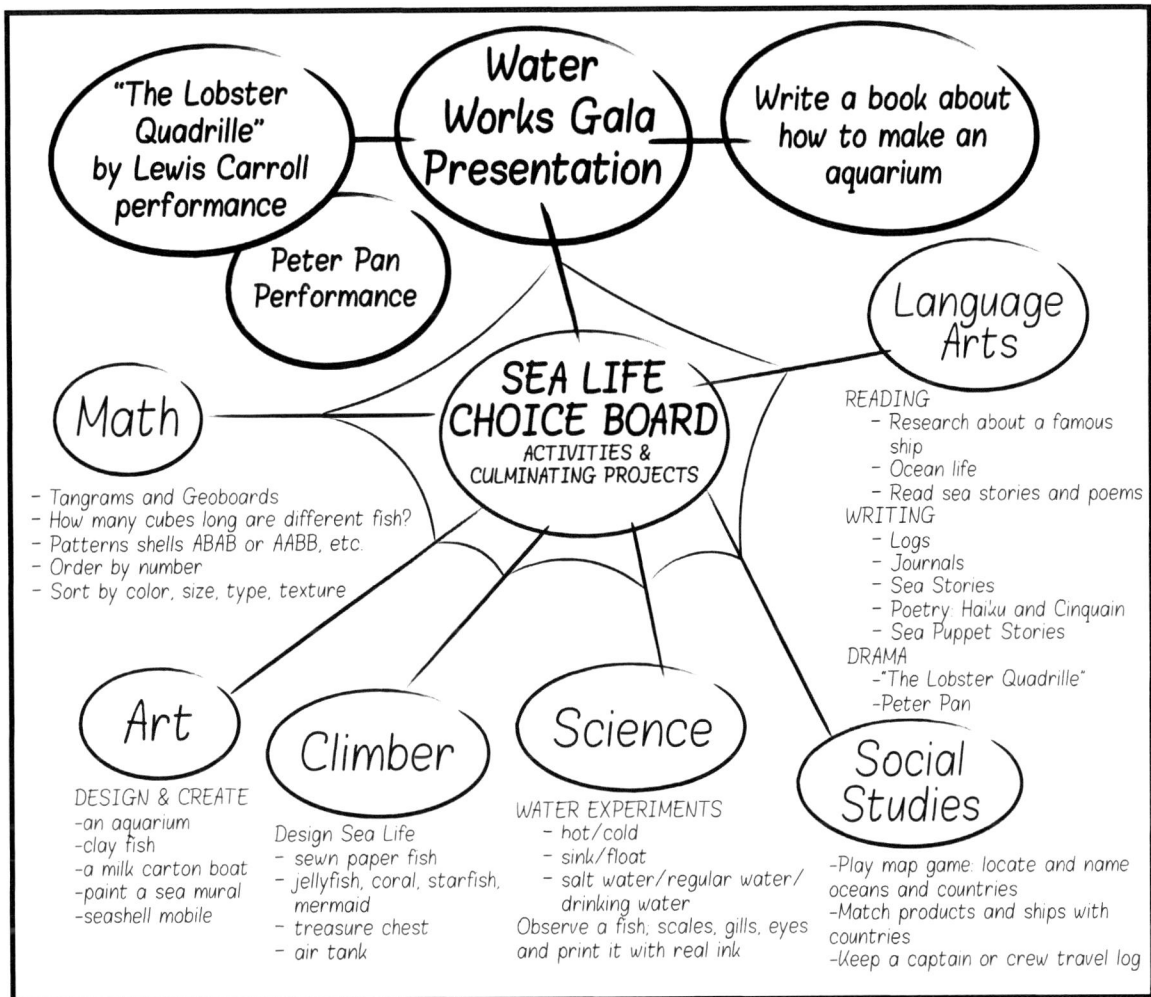

A Choice Board provides culminating activities to be chosen for the Sea Life curriculum.

Sea Life Theme Choice Board Activities for Creative Arts

We had a range of activities for Choice Board creative arts. We created our sea mural using different art mediums and then used the mural to learn. When it would not disturb others, we used walls outside of our classroom at the end of the hall. Children devised a game: *Where's the Sea Life?* They asked questions such as Where's the shark? Where's the whale? or Where's the conch shell?

We made a sea Pictionary-type game; students guessed what sea creature another person was drawing.

A student leads "Guess the Sea Life Creature" game.

We danced to environmental music with scarves, pretending to be jellyfish.

One of the favorite Choice Board time activities was the climber that we turned into an aquarium. Children added part of a sunken ship and treasure box that may have been left by a pirate. The treasure chest was filled with gold and other treasures they created. We covered the outside of the climber with acetate and then integrated art by painting waves in shades of blue and green. The children made paper sea creatures and glued them onto the waves, both outside and inside. They measured, traced, cut out, sewed, and stuffed many fish patterns to hang from the crossbar of the aquarium climber.

The children wanted a diver's air tank, so an older brother, a former Integrated Day Program student, made one for us. They made props and labeled them with their own spelling such as "trezure chess" for treasure chest and "hamrhd shrk" for hammerhead shark.

A student points to a paper sea creature.

Children transform the climber into an aquarium.

Some students who chose the puppet theater put on shows inspired by mermaids and pirates.

We immersed daily songs in the Sea Life Theme. "Baby Beluga" by Raffi became our song to sing when we needed quiet. Since I love to sing and know children love music, we sang sea songs and sea chanteys. Singing became natural to the children.

We choral read "Lobster Quadrille" by Lewis Carroll as displayed on the overhead projector. I read, they repeated, and then we read together. Many children memorized the whole thing, so I asked them if they all wanted to learn it and perform for their parents. They did.

The Lobster Quadrille

"Will you walk a little faster?"
said a whiting to a snail,
"There's a porpoise close behind us, and
he's treading on my tail.
See how eagerly the lobsters and
the turtles all advance!
They are waiting on the shingle—
will you come and join the dance?
Will you, won't you, will you, won't you,
will you join the dance?
Will you, won't you, will you, won't you,
won't you join the dance?"
"You can really have no notion
how delightful it would be
When they take us up and throw us,
with the lobsters out to sea!"
But the snail replied "Too far, too far!" and gave a
look askance
Said he thanked the whiting kindly,
but he would not join the dance.
Would not, could not, would not, could not, would
not join the dance.
Would not, could not, would not, could not, could
not join the dance.
"What matters it how far we go?"
his scaly friend replied.
"There is another shore, you know,
upon the other side.
The farther off from England
the nearer is to France—
Then turn not pale, beloved snail,
but come and join the dance.
Will you, won't you, will you, won't you,
will you join the dance?
Will you, won't you, will you, won't you,
won't you join the dance?"

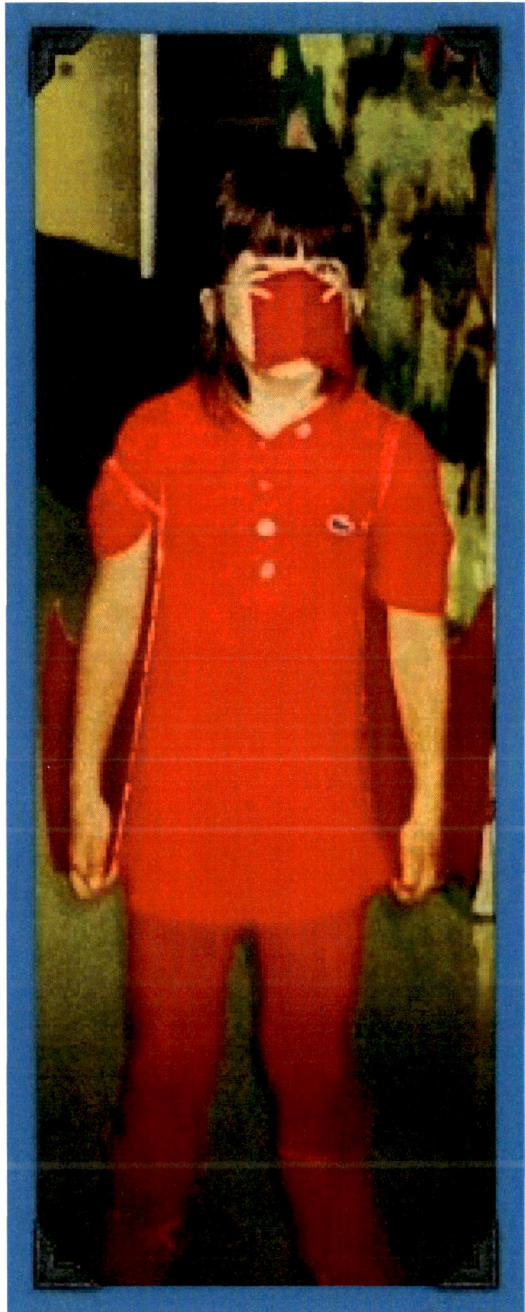

A child wears a costume
inspired by "The Lobster Quadrille."

I never would have chosen something so difficult for them to learn, but because they wanted to and were invested, learn it they did. We made simple paper masks for costumes.

The children wanted some of the songs and poems we created printed for their warmup during SSR. We wrote rhyming poems together and took turns in the author's chair or some days, we partner-read the poems. Kindergartners made a book modeled on *Brown Bear, Brown Bear* except with different colored fish and sea life.

We changed the words to "Little Miss Muffet" to include our theme in a sing-along fashion. Sea language was alive through playing, reading, writing and creating most of the day. Students acted out motions using the rhythm to "Ring around the Rosie," as in "Snail, snail, snail, snail / Go around and round

"Little Miss Muffet" takes on a fresh, fish-themed tone
after children transform the nursery rhyme.

Storytelling

The teacher starts a story and then passes a sea object to another child who adds to the story. In another version, one child picks up a shell, tells part of the story then passes to the next child, who picks up a different shell or another sea object and continues the story. In another option, each child retells the story, as the child puts back his or her shell or sea object in the center.

Variations to Storytelling

Students write about a favorite story they just heard or make up their own.

Students make a sequence puzzle book and add sequence directions: over, next, under, or on.

Students make different sized fish and put them in order according to size. Then they tell a story using size (classification) as part of the story.

A teacher can adapt Jack Prelutsky's poem "Halloween Countdown" to sea animals and sequence. Then students read and act out as a class.

> There are ten ghosts in the pantry,
> There are nine upon the stairs,
> There are eight ghosts in the attic,
> There are seven on the chairs . . . .
> Doing things that ghosts will do,
> There is one ghost right behind me
> Who is oh so quiet . . . BOO!

Students perform sequence of things that a fish, diver, ship captain, sailor, or a fisherman does. They can add interest by pretending the sea is calm, choppy, or stormy. They can discuss the performance with the audience and ask "What happened first? Next? Last?"

Students dramatize life cycles in nature such as frog, egg mass, or tadpole.

The teacher can make a version of *Pictionary* so that children dramatize and guess what is being dramatized.

Teachers can use storytelling activities to incorporate imagination, drama, and language play into transitions, calendar time, or attendance-taking.

and round." They used learned animated motions while reciting the poem to the beat of the song to create a powerful effect in control and form. We changed lyrics to songs such as "I Love the Mountains" to "I Love the Ocean."

Language Arts Sea Life Choice Board Activities

The Creative Arts and Language Arts were closely woven together in our study. We transformed our class library with genres related to sea life that included a reference materials section filled with science books. In the reference section, students learned how to use an index and a glossary, an atlas, a big book about whales, and one about all kinds of fish. The library had a section with fiction and nonfiction books at varying reading levels about the sea and even a section for student-made songbooks!

**Sea Life
Creative Arts
Choice Board Activities**

shell painting

shell magnets

shell necklaces

shell chimes

milk carton ships

dioramas

sea Colorforms (for windows)

painting

clay projects

mural

paper stuffed fish

The section they liked best included books I purchased at tag sales because they could bring them home to read with their parents.

The notes we kept on our sea research in our Sea Life notebook eventually became a published book. We shared information orally so everyone in the class could learn. We made a word list, and the words could be found all over the room because students needed them for writing and practice in spelling correctly. We made an octopus using family word strips for phonic-spelling practice. We read many sea poems and wrote some of our own. Our classroom was a literacy sea wonder.

Science Sea Life Ideas

Students brought in special artifacts and shared them, worked on a computer program about the sea, and explored scientific concepts and the experiment process. Science and the Sea Life Theme go hand-in-hand for learning. We talked about pollution of the sea and how it affects food sources. Children observed a real, no-longer-living rainbow trout. We learned about different types of water: salt water, lake water, river water, and water we drink. We took a student's plastic boat, left it in water, and noticed how the plastic didn't change over time. The children felt their classroom was theirs, and they demonstrated a "We-can-do" and an "I-can-do" attitude.

A real rainbow trout skin serves as a subject in science. Children weighed and measured it in math. They printed it in art with real printer ink.

Math Sea Life Ideas

When integrating math with a play theme, the learning objective required little time to explain because students used real-life situations and objects to manipulate. Students observed two different-sized real fish in science and used a Venn diagram in math to chart differences in measurement, weight, color, texture, differences in features, and more. We used tangrams to design fish shapes or boats, and then children wrote number-story problems about them.

Science Sea Life Choice Board Ideas

Material Objects

- collect shells, then count, sort, and classify

Aquatic Life

- observe rainbow trout including attributes such as textures, scales, eyes, gills, fins, tail
- identify kind of fish through attributes
- measure the rainbow trout length and size of fins
- observe fish scales

Water Properties and Physics

- experiment with how items sink and float with and without salt
- understand water properties and forms
- print a fish and measure how long it is using tiles
- research and answer the animal questions on Learning Web
- observe the effects of speed in water
- learn about how water wheels work
- experiment with water absorbing, repelling, and magnifying
- create tubes of water to listen to different sounds made when depth of water differs from tube to tube
- consider the effect of adding things to water such as salt, sugar, pepper, soap, dirt, and sand
- conduct experiments that focus on erosion

Scientific Process

- experiment with variables: predict, observe, and record outcomes

Crystals

- observe ice melting and freezing
- observe the effects of temperature and insulation
- observe whether a substance sinks or floats

Math Sea Life Choice Board Ideas

Measuring and Graphing

- graph properties of jellyfish using pictographs and graph paper grids
- weigh and measure the real rainbow trout with balance scales
- measure liquid using measured and labeled metric and standard-sized containers
- calculate non-standard measurement: how many shells long is __?
- measure materials needed to prepare the aquarium, make the mural, and make our fish headbands
- write word problems and stories about adding and subtracting fish
- match numerals to sets of sea-related objects
- draw fish and ships with Cuisenaire rods and add the totals
- measure the length of a ship and whale in school buses

Numbers and Math Concepts

- cut out fish or shells from paper to create patterns in a mural
- make a shell shake game used like dice with glued numerals inside: shake, open and add the numbers/math fact
- compare more and less while playing number games using fish
- write numerals 0-20 in kindergarten and 20-plus in grade one
- make a deck of fish facts
- sing fish counting songs
- participate in the shell probability exercise: predict how many shells would fall on a red fish and then find out
- count and construct sets by ones, twos, and fives
- devise fish problems for addition or subtraction

Geometry

- make Geoboard designs of fish, ships, and shells with elastics, and then record what was made on graph paper
- create tangram designs of boats and even some fish
- estimate how many tiles would fit on our cut-out fish, cover the fish, and then count the tiles

Sea Life Theme Choice Board Activities for Social Studies

By studying maps and drawing pictures, children learn about products in foreign countries.

We looked at atlases and studied maps to name and locate oceans and places where our ships traveled. One of the children had a Lego model of a plastic ship that came apart, so we learned about parts of a ship. Children investigated countries where ships originated and found facts about customs in those countries. We integrated social studies liberally into the content of reading and writing. We studied where fish and shell animals live.

We took a trip to Mystic Aquarium. We welcomed a guest speaker to our classroom to share her husband's hobby of shipbuilding. She loaned us a video about tall ships. A few children elected to watch it during Choice Board time and drew pictures of some of the ships. She gave us a replica to keep of a Maine fishing boat. Our room was getting packed.

Sea Life Culminating Experience

Finally, we were ready for the "Waterworks Gala Performance." Each child chose to present something we had learned about. We moved the mural, the aquarium climber, and all games to the cafeteria. I showed them their areas; they set up their materials and prepared for their activity. There was no time to practice. It was a live, improvised performance.

They transformed the cafeteria into a sea aquarium filled with stations: shells displayed neatly on shelves in sand and handmade Colorforms fish displayed on windows. The children hung posters both professional and

A student shows a model boat he made.

child made. They lined up their 3-D ships of recycled materials and hung or displayed mobiles. A school of handmade, patterned fish decorated the bulletin board.

We invited all of the classes in school and asked teachers to take their classes to a station that wasn't crowded. Classes saw different experiments: Can it sink or float? Is it hot or cold? The visitors interacted with children pointing out on the map where their ships might travel and other children explaining a researched fact about a country.

Visitors had a chance to do mathematical estimations such as "How many drops of water can fit on the head of a penny?"

They played the mural game, asking guests questions: "Can you find the conch shell?"

Some children danced to environmental music using scarves as waves. A presentation explained about how water gets from a reservoir to houses. My students demonstrated the process using a model they made from PVC pipes. Our guests watched children pretend to scuba dive for a hidden treasure in the pretend aquarium.

Visitors saw a display of patterned paper fish woven with streamers and clay fish hangings, all designed by the children. There was excitement. Everyone was in play mode, and the children felt empowered.

Students engage in Sea Life activities at the Waterworks Gala Performance.

Our evening Waterworks Gala Performance was the same as our day performance, except only parents and families were invited. Our treasure box at the bottom of the aquarium brimmed with prizes and goodies; all of the participants, including siblings, were able to "dive" for a treasure. As our finale, we performed "The Lobster Quadrille" ending with well-deserved applause.

The sea-themed unit was more than a splashing success. The children's play was varied and rich. We measured extensive learning in core subjects by the children's ability to be experts and share their knowledge. Each child

Children wear costumes for our Waterworks Gala Performance.

interwove the creative arts of drama, music, art, and dance with language arts, science, math, and social studies, all in a play environment. In such an active classroom, they produced quality work, interconnected many concepts, had fun with their peers, and demonstrated their love of learning.

Sample Sea Life Theme Vocabulary
General
sink, float, waves, fluid, shape, wet, absorb, freeze, melt, iceberg, steam, water vapor, rain, snow, hail, moisture, misty, crystals
storms (hurricanes, tornadoes, tsunamis)

Water Places
major oceans, North Pole, South Pole
sea, river, reservoir, stream, creek, waterfall, puddle

Shells
shiny, pretty, conch, moon shell, clams, oysters, types

Boats
bow, stern, deck, above deck, cabins, below deck, mast
captain, navigator, crew, sailors

Body Movements
spread/close, grow/shrink, dive/rise, swim left/swim right
steer left/steer right, direct north/direct south

Moving with Songs and Drama

I used large chart paper for copying songs and poems for reading. We adapted many simple rhythms from children's songs, so they could use them for play or for a puppet show in the aquarium. For example, "The Little Turtle" made an easy puppet show because a plot is implicit in the song. They just expanded the situation or changed the character to a fish or a whale.

There was a little turtle,
He lived in a box.
He swam in a puddle,
He climbed upon the rocks.
He snapped at a mosquito.
He snapped at a flea.

He snapped at a minnow,
And he snapped at me.
He caught the mosquito,
He caught the flea
He caught the minnow;
But he didn't catch me!

Other Songs Easy to be Adapted to a Theme

Original Song	*Adapted Version*
Bee, bee, bumble bee	*Shark, shark in the sea*
Stung a man upon his knee	*Nipped a man upon his knee*
Stung a man upon his snout	*Nipped a man upon his snout*
I declare that you are out.	*I declare you better get out.*
Bow, wow, wow.	*Blub, blub, blub.*
	(any noise the child chooses)

Whose dog art thou?
Little Tommy Tucker's dog.
Bow, wow, wow.
Bye, baby bunting
Daddy's gone a-hunting
To catch a little rabbit skin
To wrap the baby bunting in.

Whose fish art thou?
Little (child's name) fish
Blub, blub, blub.
Bye, baby bunting.
Daddy's gone a-fishing.
To catch a little tuna fish (or any fish)
To feed my baby bunting.

Cuckoo, in the clock
Won't you come out when I knock?
Lady, lady, buy a broom for my baby.
Sweep it low, sweep it high,
Sweep the cobwebs out of the sky.
Lady, lady, buy a broom for my baby.
Jelly in a bowl, jelly in a bowl.
Wiggle, waggle, wiggle, waggle.
Jelly in a bowl.

Cuckoo Catfish, in the sea
Won't you swim up and see me?
Lady, lady, ride a wave for my baby.
Ride it low, ride it high
Sweep the wave up to the sky,
Lady, lady, ride a wave for my baby.
A jellyfish in the ocean.
Wiggle, waggle, wiggle, waggle.
Jellyfish in the sea.

Sea Life Theme Poetry

I shared student-authored poems written by former first-grade students.
Students used them to notice and talk about what makes a poem.

The Blue Crab
Blue, green, brown, and red
Looking for food
Under the sea
Eats fish
Can walk sideways
Regrows his legs
Always moving
Best at walking backwards
—Marianne, age 6

Red Fish
Red in color
Eating seaweed
Driving up and down
Floating around the sea
It can swim well
Splashing little splashes
Helping other fish
—Brad, age 7

Bluefish
Blue and silver
Living in the sea
Under the waves
Eating little fish
Fishing for fish all day
In the ocean
Swimming
Hiding from big fish
—Amanda, age 6

Angel Fish
Always bumping into each other
Needs darkness
Gives good health for others
Eats special night food
Likes to be with the swordtail
Friendly with the other angel fish
In the seaweed
Striped or black
Has fins like angel wings
—Rebekah, age 7

The Eel
Easy to slither out of a band
Eating big fish
Living in a dark place
—Heather, age 6

Rainbow Fish
Red, orange, yellow
And green, blue, purple
In the ocean
Never to be seen
By a bird
Often eats seaweed
Water is his home
Fast swimmer
In the tropical water
Sleeps by a rock
Happy to be in the ocean.
—Peter, age 7

Sea Life Theme Poetry

We read a variety of published poems.

When Fishes Set Umbrellas Up
When fishes set umbrellas up
If the rain-drops run,
Lizards will want their parasols
To shade them from the sun.
—Christina Rossetti

By the Sea
The wide and curling ocean
Is full of splendid things
Like crabs and jellyfishes,
And weed in dripping springs,
And rocks in funny patterns,
And shells like colored foam
And barnacles and turtles
How do I get 'em home?
— Marchette Chute

Crabs
Under the water
Close to the shore,
I see two crabs walking
Across the sea floor.
They seem in a hurry,
They run without stopping,
All business and bustle,
Like ladies out shopping
—Mary E. Winchester

At the Seaside
When I was down beside the sea
A wooden spade they gave to me
To dig the sandy shore
My holes were empty like a cup
In every hole the sea came up
Till it could come no more.
—Robert Louis Stevenson

Aquarium
Colorful as butterflies,
Patterned, jewel-bright,
Are the fish in my aquarium
Snippets of rainbow light.
Blue and silver, black and gold.
Over coral ledges
They flit through fronds of greenery
Like fireflies in the hedges.
Tirelessly they glide and dart
And chase each other tails-
Fish with curious stripes and spots
Or flowing angel veils,
Tiny, perfect creatures in
This miniature sea.
Through the glass I look at them
And they look back at me.
— Ethel Jacobson

Waves
The sea is strange-
Always in motion,
In a state of change.
What is the wave
That the wind can take
The waters and make
The shape of a wave-
What is a wave
That it can break
On the shore and then
Return to the sea
To be shaped again
Into a wave?
—Mary Britton Miller

Selected Sea Life Bibliography

Agard, John, and Adrienne Kennaway. *Lend Me Your Wings*. Boston: Little, Brown, 1987.

Beck, Horace Palmer. *Folklore and the Sea*. Middletown, CT: Published for the Marine Historical Association, Mystic Seaport, by Wesleyan UP, 1973.

Bernath, Stefan, and James W. Atz. *Tropical Fish Coloring Book*. New York: Dover Publications, 1978.

Berne, Eric. *Games People Play*. New York: Grove Press, Inc., 1964.

Carr, Marion Bergner. *The Golden Picture Book of Sea and Shore: Tide Pools, Shells, Small Animals, the Big and Little Creatures of the Ocean; Tides, Currents, Islands, and Other Wonders of the Sea*. New York: Golden, 1959.

Cavoukian, Raffi, and Ashley Wolff. *Baby Beluga*. New York: Crown, 1992.

Chock, Eric. "What Can I Say?" *Small Kid Time Hawaii*. Bamboo Ridge Press.

Cosgrove, Stephen, and Robin James. *Maui-Maui*. Los Angeles, CA: Price/Stern/Sloan, 1979.

Coulombe, Deborah A. *The Seaside Naturalist: A Guide to Nature Study at the Seashore*. Englewood Cliffs, NJ: Prentice-Hall, 1984.

Darby, Gene. *What Is a Fish*. Chicago: Benefic, 1958.

Douglass, Jackie Leatherbury and John Douglass. *A Field Guide to Shells Coloring Book*. Boston, MA: Houghton Mifflin, 1985.

Ganeri, Anita. *Wonder of the Sea*. London: Publiprint, 2012.

Granowsky, Alvin, and Dan McGuirk. *The Seahorse*. London: Macmillan Education, 1984.

Hall, Mary Ann, and Catherine Minor. *Take a Bite of Music, It's Yummy!* New England Association for the Education of Young Children, 1982.

Hanauer, Ethel R. *Biology Experiments for Children*. New York: Dover Publications, 1968.

Helmreich, Stefan. *Alien Ocean: Anthropological Voyages in Microbial Seas*. Berkeley: University of California, 2009.

King, Patricia. *Mabel, the Whale*. Chicago: Follett Pub., 1958.

Kinney, Jean Brown., and Cle Kinney. *What Does the Tide Do?* New York: Young Scott, 1966.

Lionni, Leo. *Swimmy*. New York: Pantheon, 1963.

Makedon, Alexander. *John Dewey's Views on Science and Play in Education*. *http://alexandermakedon.com/articles/JohnDewy.html*. Chicago State University, 1991.

McGovern, Ann, and John Hamberger. *Little Whale*. New York: Four Winds, 1979.

O'Neill, Mary Le Duc, and Leonard Weisgard. *Hailstones and Halibut Bones: Adventures in Color*. Garden City, NY: Doubleday, 1961.

Pansini, Anna, and Renzo Barto. *"I Wonder Why."* Mahwah, NJ: Troll Associates, 1991.

Phleger, Fred B., and Paul Galdone. *The Whales Go by*. New York: Beginner Book, 1959.

Platt, Rutherford Hayes. *Walt Disney's Worlds of Nature; a Treasury of True-life Adventures*. New York: Simon and Schuster, 1957.

Podendorf, Illa, and Mary Gehr. *Pebbles and Shells*. Chicago: Children's, 1972.

Ramsbottom, Edward, Joan Redmayne, and Roy Spencer. *Streams and Rivers*. London: Macmillan, 1977.

Rius, María and José María Parramón. *Life in the Sea*. New York: Barron's, 1987.

Weno, John Bonnet. *Whales*. Zoobooks Series. 1983.

Williams, Vera B., and Jennifer Williams. *Stringbean's Trip to the Shining Sea*. New York: Greenwillow, 1988.

Zeman, Ludmila. *Sindbad: From the Tales of The Thousand and One Nights*. Toronto: Tundra, 1999.

An Imagination-Inspired Childhood

The creation of something new is not accomplished by the intellect but by the play instinct.

—Carl Jung

For a life to exist presents a mystery in itself. A child has the ability to create and express what sets human beings apart from other living creatures. In order to realize one's self, an individual must develop mind, body, and imagination. A child who gradually develops creative capacities feels competent to meet, rather than fear, environmental forces of daily living. The child becomes a resourceful, confident individual capable of finding a way to meet varying circumstances.

Furthermore, when children trust and develop imagination, they use inner vision in five areas of living: physical environment, unexpected situations, ability to understand and express ideas and how to share them, appreciating solitude, and recognizing interactions.

The first area imagination strengthens is the ability to interact in the physical environment to learn and grow. In order to be secure in the area of concrete objects, a child must learn to create tactically and make things. Each child must have opportunities for dreaming and creating, then applying ideas while kinesthetically engaged.

If we want children to respect their physical environment, they need to help build it. For example, in my classroom I had a wooden climber with a loft with rope and wooden ladders on either side. The students enjoyed coming up with ideas about what we could turn the climber into for each thematic unit. They respected it and once turned it into a hut for a *Three Little Pigs* play. The students owned the climber and took care not to wreck it.

Everything in the classroom is a tool students may use and create with. There is a difference between giving students a lesson on using scissors and asking them to cut paper on dotted lines for no purpose or asking them to cut out a sail for the mast for a sailboat. Planning, measuring, and drawing the mast must happen before the cutting begins. Students then see scissors as a tool for creating and will take care of the useful tool. In the end, a clear purpose will make the difference between successful lessons and unsuccessful lessons.

A second way imagination helps in life involves meeting unexpected situations. Knowing how to deal with a problem by figuring out an alternative allows children to feel safe. Imagination contributes to emotional stability and the security of others. A child can save a situation from becoming an emotional calamity. The child becomes resourceful and gradually develops a perceptive attitude toward solving problems and meeting unexpected situations or emergencies. Within, a child gains a secure attitude, remains calm, and figures out what to do. Providing opportunities for students to engage in play gives them a chance to learn who they are through imagination.

A third area of living strengthened by imagination involves a child's ability to understand and express ideas and opinions. A creative person has power to visualize, picture, and understand a situation. The ability to perceive allows an individual to express opinions, contribute to a plan of action, and consider values. Additionally, imagination aids in how one expresses ideas to others so another person may consider, accept, and discuss them. A sense of security results when a child shares thoughts.

Lacking imagination leads to few ideas or opinions generated or even borrowed from others. Without imagination, a child fears speaking or sharing ideas and opinions. Lack of imagination leads to an inability to explain or clarify one's ideas, thoughts, and convictions. Imagination provides an internal initiative to move ahead with ideas and express them.

A fourth way imagination helps in life results in a person's ability to enjoy solitude, even when with others. People need to be alone from time to time. For personal satisfaction, the creative spirit needs refreshing. Imagination provides an individual with satisfying avenues for personal enjoyment. When one's thoughts are constantly invaded, unhappiness prevails and a person begins to depend on commercialized amusements that result in lack of vision and drive to do something that synchronizes the whole being. When an individual nourishes and exercises imaginative faculties in childhood and thereafter, he or she sustains creativity throughout life.

Just as imagination builds one's appreciation of time spent by oneself, it also strengthens social relationships. Each person needs a creative attitude to nurture concern for others and with others. Through imagination, the child empathizes and brightens the lives of others, which leads to friendships. Happiness spreads, furthering the true spirit of living.

Imagination builds avenues of understanding. When a child shares imagination with a parent, the parent will identify with the child, which leads to understanding. Imagination prepares for new experiences. A child playing, acting out, and imagining a new experience enjoys rather than fears the experience. The same applies in school.

Emotion is one of the strongest forces to nourish creative appreciation. John Dewey writes that creativity must be encouraged in education. He explains that aesthetic appreciation begins with sensitive awareness to the harmonies and beauties in the environment, which leads to being able to create.

Awareness of the environment develops imagination through the emotion and senses: sight, smell, taste, touch, and hearing. Awareness of one's senses transfers to nature. When children become sensitive to beauty in nature, they become more sensitive to their own relationships with human nature. Recognizing and accepting the beauty in one's self and others then leads to respect for one's community, the world we know, and beyond. Imagination connects every word, thought, and action. Imagination is play with ideas and feelings. Imagination is magic. Schools can be classrooms of magic at work.

One of my favorite ancient Chinese proverbs is *A child's life is like a piece of paper on which every person makes a mark.* Every person, whether directly in our lives or not, affects us all, something adults who guide young children must always remember.

As teachers, we have a part in mixing the bread batter, the young child's love of life. We must be careful not to stifle their lives' energy by separating behaviors into discrete parts. We must allow the batter to rise with infusions of living, enjoying, and trusting that each being is a part of the greatness of life itself.

In this day of rapidly escalating technology and information, we can no longer minimize the power of play.

Meaningful play assures learning mastery.
Play is empowering. It is self-chosen.

It internalizes and develops problem solving, imagination, individual strengths, social skills, physical prowess, spiritual enthusiasm, cognitive growth, and aesthetic awareness. It is highly self-motivating.

It is unusually flexible and open, yet follows ever changing and readily adaptable rules.

We can all share in the magic of play.
—MaryJane Devlin

Acknowledgments

from Susan Argyros and Elizabeth Devlin

We would like to thank Mrs. Devlin's former students Mary, Ellie, Chris, Alea, Matt, Jeff, Cougar, Christie (your sand dollar is on the cover), and Patrick (who had his boat twenty years later) for sharing fond memories of their Integrated K-1 experiences with us.

We would also like to thank Mrs. Devlin's former colleagues: Laura Powell, for sending us the original *Integrated Day Handbook* and Dan and MaryJane Hesford for sharing stories of our mom and sending videos of the Integrated Day program and a televised interview. A thank you to Cynthia Weisslender, who also taught in the ID program, for reviewing the book. A very special thank you to Alicia Sturgess, who worked with our mother and shared her insider's view of the class in action.

A thank you to Peter Lund for his encouragement to write our mom's story and to Eileen Lawton for reading through the early manuscript with us on a Friday night. Appreciation to Ana Devlin-Gauthier for her help with the web page.

A special thank you to Ariana and Nicholas Argyros, kindergarteners at the time, for using their great-grandmother's folded paper technique to write stories so we could have examples.

A heartfelt thank you to our niece-in-law Christin Wilson Devlin for her artistic talent, her ability to envision our mother's story playfully, and her constant positive outlook.

To Marcia Gagliardi of Haley's Publishing . . . we are deeply grateful to you for embracing our mom's story about play and educating young people. We appreciate your commitment and countless hours to this endeavor.

A big shout-out to our families, who understood the hours and years we spent were out of love of our mother and her love (and ours) for teaching.

Thank you to David for his endless support.

(continued next page)

(continued from previous page)

Our biggest thank you goes to our dad, Lee Devlin, who shared his own stories about when he volunteered in the Integrated Day K-1 and especially for his continued care, encouragement, and support throughout this project.

Lastly, thank you to our mom, MaryJane Devlin, who believed every one of her students was smart, curious, and gifted with unlimited potential; who believed teaching requires dedication and hard work; and who believed all learning must be meaningful, engaging, and full of play.

Reflections on the Timelessness of Play and Learning

an afterword by Elizabeth Devlin

What started out to be a gift of our mother's legacy to her family turned into an unexpected gift to me as an elementary teacher. My sister Susan started digging through hundreds of pages of our mother's drafts, notes, and artifacts. She slipped into our mother's shoes to channel her voice while crafting the text. Susan kept feeding me morsels of our mother's message and asking me to join the journey. Despite my reluctance, my sister's passion pulled me in to help realize our mother's dream and share it. Although working on *The Power of Play and Learning* as a daughter was done with the highest regard for our mother's contributions, paralleling that work was a professional question that quietly niggled at me and made me reticent: Was our mother's work relevant twenty years later in this millennium?

By suspending my judgment on what was missing from our mother's text, I uncovered the the timelessness of her message for childhood and primary education. I uncovered what many teachers have kept as vital to early childhood education: child development, child-centered curriculum, multi-sensory experiences, and play. I uncovered a lens to use to reflect on my own practice.

My working on *The Power of Play and Learning* came at a time when I was in the middle of an educational experience that seemed to be in a different context from our mother's. Where in her story were the acronyms and terminology that have become part of a school's language? Where were anti-bias and multi-cultural curriculum, CCSS, MCAS, RtI, formative or performance assessment, writing process, workshop, PBL, PBIS, SE, ESL, rubrics, responsive classroom, habits of mind, restorative practice, growth mindset, and other such nomenclature? As I delved deeper into the writing of our mother's philosophy and practice, the through lines presented themselves across decades and children. Her approaches remain relevant to education and children in the twenty-first century.

When children negotiate while sharing experiences and goals, they can develop caring relationships with culturally or racially diverse children. When teachers set up child-centered classrooms and learning experiences facilitated for everyone, they create opportunities for a highly engaging and accessible curriculum. By hypothesizing and revising through trial and error where mistakes are seen as opportunities for learning, children experience and develop growth mindsets. Partner and class meetings to problem-solve, empathize, share, and care set up a climate similar to experiences of restorative circles. Choice allows children, individually and together, to be leaders of their learning. The message is *You are developing and can learn.* The message was not *You are below or above benchmark.*

Yes, our mother's insights written more than twenty years ago have a place in childhood and education in 2018. Involving children in setting up their environments holds them accountable for taking care of their environments. Children setting their goals, then evaluating their work through play, artifacts, and reflection is authentic assessment. The Sea Life Gala Performance is a performance assessment especially remarkable in its own right, given that the children were in kindergarten and first grade. Theme-based learning is linked to project-based learning. The list goes on.

There are many possible links to connective neuroscience. Children fully engaged, retrieving information, and building knowledge network parts of the brain from the frontal cortex across hemispheres and the heart of the brain, the amygdala. All of it leads to long-term memory, caring beings, and self care.

Our mother's insights are as relevant in 2018 as they were twenty years ago. I hope *The Power of Play and Learning* has been a gift that you will unwrap again and again when you want to refresh your outlook on childhood as a time to hope, imagine, inquire, problem-solve, invent, and create . . . as a powerful frontier of play, learning, and caring.

About the Authors

MaryJane Devlin worked at Abraham Pierson and Lewin Joel School in Clinton, Connecticut, for more than thirty years as a teacher of kindergarten and first grade. She was co-founder of an initiative for a school-within-a school program called Integrated Day, where she worked for half her career. She received many grants for innovative teaching curricula and practices. She often spoke at area colleges. MaryJane lives with her husband, Lee, in Clinton. They have five children, twelve grandchildren, and ten great-grandchildren.

Susan H. D. Argyros teaches English and is a literacy specialist at Exeter High School in Exeter, New Hampshire. Chosen as a finalist for the New Hampshire Council of Teachers of English Award in 2010, Susan believes, as do her mother and sister, that teaching is an honor and students' needs come first. She models her love of learning through reading and writing with her students. When not teaching, she is often found playing with her grandchildren. She lives with her family in New Hampshire.

Elizabeth Devlin has worked in education for more than twenty-five years as a classroom teacher, reading specialist, intervention teacher, and literacy coach. She has taught adult literacy and English as a second or foreign language. She teaches at Wildwood Elementary School in Amherst, Massachusetts, and serves as a teacher-consultant with the Western Massachusetts Writing Project. She believes literacy, critical thinking, imagination, and curiosity develop pathways for children to create their lives and change the world.

About the Illustrator

Christine Wilson Devlin's first illustrations can be found in *The Rock Cycle, Like a Circle,* a book she wrote and illustrated for her science class when she was in the ninth grade. The only copy resides in her personal library. She is the entrepreneur of an online boutique, 0 Inside Out. Christine lives in the state of Washington with her husband, Liam, and their cat, Gabby.

Selected Bibliography

"Abstract." *ECRP. Vol 4 No 1. The Role of Pretend Play in Children's Cognitive Development.* . 05 Sep. 2016.

Bergen, Doris, "The Role of Pretend Play in Children's Cognitive Development." *Early Childhood Research and Practice.* 2002.

Berne, Eric. *Games People Play: The Psychology of Human Relations.* Harmondsworth: Penguin, 1967.

Burton, Leon, and Kathy Kuroda. *ArtsPlay: Creative Activities in Dance, Drama, Art and Music for Young Children.* Menlo Park, CA: Addison-Wesley, 1981.

"Cat Training | Cat Behavior." *Predatory Behavior of Cats.* . 30 July 2014.

Colorado Correlations: A Correlation of Colorado's Model Content Standards with Project WILD, Aquatic WILD, Project Learning Tree and Project WET Activities Guides. Denver, CO: Colorado Division of Wildlife.

Berne, Eric, MD. "Description of Transactional Analysis and Games." 20 July 2016.

Dewey, John. "Individuality in Education." *General Science Quarterly* 7.3 (1923): 157-66.

Ekberg, Marion Hopping, and Jean Warren. *Piggyback Songs: Compiled from Songs Contributed to the Totline Newsletter.* Everett, WA: Warren, 1983.

Fiarotta, Phyllis, and Noel Fiarotta. *Snips & Snails & Walnut Whales: Nature Crafts for Children.* New York: Workman Pub., 1975.

Griswell, Kim T. *The Best of The Mailbox Magazine. Preschool/Kindergarten.* Greensboro, NC: Education Center, 1999.

Hall, Mary Ann, and Catherine Minor. *Take a Bite of Music, It's Yummy!* New England Association for the Education of Young Children, 1982.

Hanauer, Ethel, and Adeline Naiman. "Book and Film Reviews: Biology Demonstrations for Teachers and Parents: Biology Experiments for Children." *The Physics Teacher* 8.9 (1970): 539.

(continued next page)

(continued from previous page)

Koste, Jinny Glasgow. *A Time for Play: An Initiation into the Open Secrets of Play*. Ypsilanti, MI: Koste, 1976.

O'Neill, Mary Le Duc, and Leonard Weisgard. *Hailstones and Halibut Bones: Adventures in Color*. Garden City, NY: Doubleday, 1961.

PLT: Supplementary Activity Guide. Washington, D.C.: American Forest Council, 1987.

Pring, Richard. "Child-centered Education." in *John Dewey: a Philosopher of Education for our Time?* Fourth Edition. London and New York: Bloomsbury Academic, 2007.

Scheckel, Larry. *Ask a Science Teacher, How Everyday Stuff Really Works: Why Don't We Feel the Earth Spin? How Do Airplanes Stay in the Air? What Makes Blood Red? and 247 Other Things You've Always Wondered about*. New York, NY: Experiment, LLC, 2013.

Siks, Geraldine Brain. *Drama with Children*. New York: Harper & Row, 1977.

The Mailbox Preschool Magazine. www.mailbox.com. Education Center LLC.

Warren, Jean, Elizabeth McKinnon, and Marion Hopping. Ekberg. *Small World Celebrations*. Everett, WA: Warren Pub. House, 1988.

Wildsmith, Brian. *Fishes*. New York: Franklin Watts, 1968.

Zoobooks. Wildlife Education Ltd.

Colophon

Text for *The Power of Play & Learning* is set in Bookmania, a typeface designed in 2011 by Mark Simonson. Bookmania combines the sturdy elegance of the original Bookman Oldstyle, created in 1901, with the swashy exuberance of the Bookmans of the 1960s. Bookmania sports more than 680 swash characters, more than any previous Bookman. A flourish addition replacing a terminal or serif constitutes a swash character, a typographical flourish like an exaggerated serif. The broad range of Bookmania weights make it great for display use, but it also works well for text. Unlike some Bookman revivals, it retains the original classic sloped roman for the italic.

Titles for *The Power of Play & Learning* are set in the Chalkboard font released by Apple in 2003 as part of Mac OS X v10.3.